The Workshop Survival Guide

How to design and teach workshops that work every time

By Rob Fitzpatrick and Devin Hunt

All rights reserved, Robfitz Ltd, 2019

http://workshopsurvival.com

Contents

Why this book (and these authors) can help i

Part one: Workshop Design Essentials 1

Maintain goodwill with regular "a-ha" moments 3

Don't start with the slides (do start with the Skeleton) 7

Vary the Teaching Formats to improve energy, attention, and learning 32

The five essential Teaching Formats 37

Design your exercises and refine your schedule 63

Begin with the bare minimum number of slides 69

Summary of Part 1 83

Part two: Facilitation Essentials 87

How to introduce yourself without making everyone hate you 88

Don't treat your audience as bigger than it is	93
Seating and group formation	99
Getting more from your exercises	107
Answering student questions	114
How to recover the crowd after an exercise	119
Overcoming hostility, skepticism, and troublemakers	126
Staying on schedule and dealing with delays	144
Charisma can be manufactured with a clicker, a watch, and some small behaviors	152
Protect your own energy by hiding during breaks	156
Using co-teachers, expert guests, and helpers	159
What to do when everything goes wrong	166
Serve the people in the room, even if there aren't so many of them	174
Summary of Part 2 (and a facilitation checklist):	176
Conclusion and final thoughts	**179**
Appendix: Advanced Teaching Formats	182
Appendix: An example of inventing, testing, and perfecting a new exercise	203

Why this book (and these authors) can help

There are many good styles of workshops and many good ways to design them.

As such, we are in no way claiming that the approach presented in this book is the *only* way. Nor are we claiming that facilitators who are doing it differently are doing it wrong.

But we *are* claiming that this approach is a *very good* way (and possibly the best way for facilitators who are just starting out). **It's good because it's simple, it's reliable, and it works.** 'Simple' means we can tell you how to do it in a way which is concrete, understandable, and easy to implement. 'Reliable' means that it will work with every type of audience and for almost every topic and will do so every time. And we know it works because we've used this approach to teach many hundreds of workshops ourselves and have trained others to successfully do the same.

During our first ten years of teaching, we were enthusiastic amateurs: first as teaching assistants in university classrooms, and then running small workshops and lectures to share our ongoing startup experiences with other entrepreneurs. Workshops then became our full-time profession, first as freelancers and then while running a small education agency.[1]

We've now designed and run a huge number of successful workshops (and a few major flops) covering every type of audience: executives, undergrads, MBAs, disadvantaged youths, busy professionals, and more. We've designed everything from 20-minute teasers to 3-month intensives, in locations ranging from Costa Rica and Qatar to London and Berlin. We've taught for companies like HP and Deloitte and for universities like Oxford and NYU. We've built workshops for every price point, from free upskilling (paid for by the state or employer) through to $4000-per-seat premium events. We've taught casual sessions, with beer in hand and flip-flop on foot, through to formal, posh affairs with glitzy venues and high-end catering. **In every case, no matter where it was located or who it was for, the process outlined in these pages worked.**[2]

Perhaps most importantly, **we can teach you how to do this.** And you don't need to turn into some kind of charismatic superstar for it to work. In fact, you don't even need to be particularly confident. You only need to know how to design a good workshop. We've trained up teachers from scratch who are now billing upwards of £2000 per day and getting invited back to

---

[1] The agency was called Founder Centric. The other two partners were Salim Virani (who went on to found Source Institute, which designs hard-to-teach and peer-to-peer education) and Jordan Schlipf.

[2] That's not to say we've never screwed up a workshop. We have. But in each case, it was because we had messed up or misunderstood some part of the process, and, once we'd figured it out, that particular problem stopped being such a problem. By reading this book, you'll hopefully be able to avoid many of the obstacles that we ran into.

teach again and again. This stuff isn't complicated. You can learn it and you can do it.

Our goal for this book—and our promise to you—is that you'll feel comfortable designing a workshop from scratch and running it successfully, regardless of whether it's 20 minutes or two days long. You'll also be able to "fix" a broken workshop that you've been saddled with. While the first attempt at a new workshop is never perfect (testing and refinement matter), it should still be good enough that both clients and attendees leave happy, and that you get invited back. Throughout this book, you'll also gain the skills and knowledge such that if something goes wrong, you'll understand what's happening and how to fix it. Whether workshops are your whole world or just a small part of it, we can help you succeed.

Please note that this book is primarily about educational workshops, where the goal is to teach, upskill, and educate (as opposed to brainstorming or consulting workshops). Much of what we cover will apply to all varieties of workshops, but we'll only be going into the full process for the educational ones.

This book draws on both Rob and Devin's experiences. But in an attempt to keep the language simple and avoid having to constantly clarify who did what, we'll generally just merge our stories, anecdotes, and opinions into a shared first person "I".

Lastly, a word of thanks. This book wouldn't be possible without the expertise and influence of the countless wonderful people who we've had the pleasure of teaching alongside over the years. Huge thanks to all of them, and especially to Salim Virani, who was with us in the trenches for the pivotal years when we were all figuring this stuff out together.

How to use this book

Part 1 covers the essentials of workshop design, which includes picking precisely what to teach, designing brilliant exercises, and figuring out your schedule. It's all the stuff you do beforehand to make the day itself as easy and successful as possible.

Part 2 covers the essentials of facilitation. It starts with how to introduce yourself and then continues to the challenge of how to smoothly form groups, run exercises, and recover the crowd's attention. We'll also look at dealing with bad luck, hostile crowds, hostile individuals, slipped schedules, and more.

The Appendix contains a few advanced approaches to designing specialized workshop exercises.

Let's get into it.

Part one:
Workshop Design Essentials

Every workshop lives or dies by two factors:
- What the audience learns
- How the audience feels (i.e. energy and attention)

Compared to a traditional class or lecture, a workshop has two special qualities. The first is that instead of *expecting* the audience to pay attention, you'll be taking responsibility for their energy and attention by designing the session in a way which continually renews and refreshes them. By working to boost their energy, you'll also boost their ability to pay attention, which ultimately makes it easier for them to learn.

"Attention is the first step in the learning process. We cannot understand, learn or remember that which we do not first attend to."

—*CDL, Center for Development & Learning*[3]

The other special quality of a workshop is that you're able to coordinate *what* you're teaching with *how* you teach it. Or in other words, you have the opportunity to escape the constraints of the lecture and start picking the styles of teaching and types of exercises best suited to the topic at hand. Imagine showing up to a yoga class where the instructor put you in a chair, lectured for an hour, and then told you to go home and practice. You'd be mad! And that's exactly how lots of lectures end up feeling. Lectures work fine for delivering pure "book knowledge", but are terrible for teaching anything involving skills, wisdom, evaluation, practice, decision-making, and judgement.

We'll get to the question of facilitation in Part 2. But I want to be clear that **the crux of a brilliant workshop lies in what you do beforehand.** When a workshop is well-designed, it does most of the heavy lifting for you, and facilitation becomes naturally easy. On the other hand, all the fancy facilitation tricks in the world still won't save you if you haven't properly designed the foundation.

---

[3] https://www.cdl.org/attention/

Maintain goodwill with regular "a-ha" moments

Most workshops begin with the audience liking you. You have their goodwill, they trust you, and you're credible. It's like the suspension of disbelief in sci-fi and fantasy movies: people show up *wanting* to be entertained, so they're happy to suspend their skepticism and go along with some crazy shenanigans. But if the movie goes too far and becomes laughable, the suspension snaps and the viewers become hostile. The same is true for your audience's goodwill.

You can think of goodwill as a consumable (and renewable) resource:

- You *lose* goodwill whenever you make the audience sit through boring stuff (like a long intro) or participate in low-value exercises (like an off-topic icebreaker[4])

---

[4] You almost certainly don't need (or want) an icebreaker. If the icebreaker's goal is for attendees to meet and get comfortable with each other, then why not allow them to do so during an exercise which also carries an educational payload?

- You *gain* goodwill whenever you deliver a nugget of value (usually in the form of a valuable "a-ha" moment or takeaway)

Some time ago, I attended a one-hour talk about innovation strategy at a beach resort on the Adriatic Sea.[5] Folks were excited to be there, and goodwill was high. The teacher began with some powerful insights about what was and wasn't innovation. Plus, he was charismatic, funny, and was live-sketching his own talk, which was certainly neat to watch. He soon started asking questions to the audience: "Who remembers this? Who had one of these? Raise your hands." For the next 45 minutes, he entertained, but didn't deliver any more big takeaways until the very end. He had still been sketching and making jokes through that middle stretch, but he hadn't *taught* anything in ages. So each time he asked the audience another question, fewer hands went up until he eventually found himself making futile requests to a dead room. That's goodwill drain in action.

The unspoken contract of a workshop is this: the audience grants you temporary control of their attention (and actions) in the belief that you will transmute it into something new and valuable. If you violate this contract by asking too much before returning sufficient

---

[5] I was teaching at the same event later that day. After finishing my session and walking away, I realised I'd forgotten my bag on the refreshments table up on stage. The next speaker had already begun, but the strap of my bag was hanging forwards and I figured I could retrieve it from below without causing undue interruption. But when I gave it a tug, I took down the whole table, showering the stage and front-row audience with bubbly water and broken glass. Not my slickest moment, but apparently a memorable one for the audience.

value, then they grow suspicious of your authority, their goodwill evaporates, and you lose them.
This helps explain the mistakes of the live-sketching teacher. Although he started strong, the crowd's goodwill eroded during the long delay between the big "a-ha" moments at the very start and very end of his session. (This simple matter of scheduling was the crucial mistake, which we'll learn how to prevent and fix in the upcoming sections.) His second mistake was in asking the audience to do tasks which didn't return meaningful insight. Participating in his hand-raising requests didn't create additional value for participants, so people simply stopped responding. And as a side effect, they became distrustful of his authority and less willing to engage in future tasks. It's worth pointing out that this facilitator was both experienced and competent.[6] But at the event I attended, he got so lost in the razzle-dazzle that he overlooked the most essential requirement of teaching: to deliver Learning Outcomes.

Learning Outcomes are important. They're the specific bits of knowledge, skill, or insight that your audience takes away. They're the difference between what someone knows (and can do) when they arrive compared to what they know (and can do) when they leave. They're the reason folks have bothered showing up.
For goodwill to remain high, you must quickly and consistently deliver value. Once you've started doing so, the audience will be conditioned to believe that when you ask them to do something weird, it's going

---

[6] He was actually really great and I feel a bit bad for picking on a single example of his work. (I've certainly given far worse performances, as YouTube can confirm.) Plus, he was constrained by a bad room setup (fixed-row auditorium) which made exercises hard to run. But that doesn't mean we can't learn from the result.

to end up being awesome, so they'll be responsive and high-energy about pretty much everything. When goodwill is low, the opposite holds: they'll respond sluggishly to facilitation requests, won't pay as much attention to lectures, and will goof around during discussions and exercises.

The best way to ensure that your frequently deliver these "a-ha" moments is to zoom out and design the fundamental building blocks first, before you worry about slides, exercises, or any of the details. Taken together, these fundamentals are called a "Workshop Skeleton", and in the next few sections, we'll learn how to put together a great one.

Lessons learned:

- Learning Outcomes are the specific, high-value takeaways that the audience has shown up for (and which they hopefully leave with)
- Attendees typically show up with high goodwill, so you just need to maintain it by quickly and consistently delivering valuable Learning Outcomes

Don't start with the slides (do start with the Skeleton)

The first thing everyone does, upon sitting down to create a workshop, is to open their presentation software and start making slides. This is a huge mistake and will ruin your workshop by trapping you in the details before you've figured out the fundamentals.

So if you've already opened your presentation software, go ahead and close it. Instead, get hold of a fresh document or a blank scrap of paper. Throughout the next few sections of this book, you're going to fill it in with the three crucial foundations of every good workshop:

1. Audience Profile — Who it's for
2. Schedule Chunks — When they get their coffee breaks
3. Learning Outcomes — What they'll take away

Or even more simply: who/when/what. Taken together, these three ingredients make up the Workshop Skeleton. The Skeleton is the day's raw structure and purpose, free of the distracting details of exactly what you and your slides will say. It looks like this:

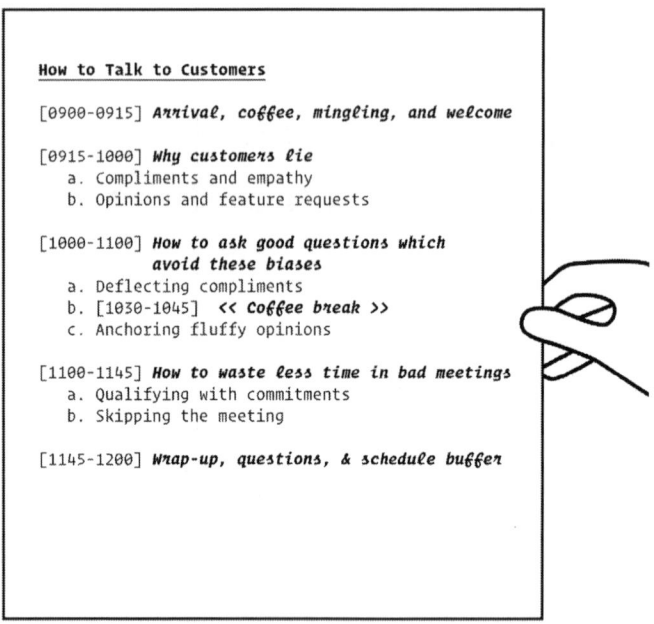

```
How to Talk to Customers

[0900-0915]  Arrival, coffee, mingling, and welcome

[0915-1000]  Why customers lie
    a. Compliments and empathy
    b. Opinions and feature requests

[1000-1100]  How to ask good questions which
             avoid these biases
    a. Deflecting compliments
    b. [1030-1045]  << Coffee break >>
    c. Anchoring fluffy opinions

[1100-1145]  How to waste less time in bad meetings
    a. Qualifying with commitments
    b. Skipping the meeting

[1145-1200]  Wrap-up, questions, & schedule buffer
```

The Workshop Skeleton is easy to create, easy to iterate, and offers a high-level view of all the stuff that matters. And it starts with the question of who is in the room.

You need to know who's in the room

One of my worst-ever workshops was in Moscow. I had shown up expecting a group of experienced entrepreneurs and had prepared my Learning Outcomes (and thus my exercises and everything else) on that assumption. But when I arrived, I found myself facing a group which was closer to 25% entrepreneurs and 75%

"curious onlookers". This was problematic. I had intended to skip all the introductory theory and leap straight into group exercises where attendees wrestled with their own business challenges. But I now had an audience full of people who not only didn't know the basics, but who didn't even have a business! Although my workshop had been well-tested and well-refined in advance, it was guaranteed to fail on this particular day because it didn't match the people in the room.

To avoid making a similar sort of blunder, it's wise to begin any design by first figuring out who it's for. Depending on the situation, the audience can be either a choice or a constraint. For example, if you're designing an event from scratch, then you're free to design toward whichever type of audience you eventually intend to invite. If, on the other hand, you've been asked to teach for a pre-existing group or event, then the audience is a fixed constraint who you'll need to learn about, understand, and design around.

Beyond avoiding blunders like my Moscow mishap, nailing down a good Audience Profile is also crucial for deciding what to include and what to cut. Imagine you've been asked to run a workshop about "sales". That's a pretty big topic! Given how many books have been written about it, you're going to have a tough time getting down to a tight couple of hours. Fortunately, there's a way to simplify since *what* you teach and *how* you teach it are based on *who* you're teaching.

As such, to decide what's "in" and what's "out", you only need to consider your audience. Toward that end, here are a few clarifying questions:

- **Who are they?** Students? Professionals? Freelancers? The strong and successful? The vulnerable and

ostracized? Is the audience all one type of person or will several different groups be present?
- **How experienced are they?** How much do they already know? Have they put it into practice or is it only theoretical? Do you need to cover the basics, or can you skip ahead?
- **Why are they bothering to show up?** What do they expect to leave with? What would make the workshop a huge "win" for them? If their boss is forcing them to attend, what does their boss want?
- **What are their concerns and objections?** Are they carrying any skepticism or prejudice about this topic which you'll need to maneuver around? Might they be worried that the topic is too trivial, too complex, or just not for them? Are they grumpy that their boss/friend/spouse forced them to show up? Are there any other likely issues?

If you're designing a session for an existing group, then discovering your Audience Profile is as simple as sending a short email to the client or event organizer:

> Hey Mark, looking forward to the session on the 27th about [topic]. Just wanted to get some details on the audience to make sure I highlight the right points.
>
> - What sort of people are going to be attending?
> - How much experience do they already have with the topic?
> - What are they hoping to get out of the day?
> - Is there anything they're likely to be skeptical or concerned about?

- From your perspective, what would make the session a big win?

And to re-confirm, is it still correct that we're looking at 50-70 attendees and a 90-minute running time? Thanks!

The main purpose of an Audience Profile is to help you decide exactly which Learning Outcomes will be relevant for the people in the room and what you can cut. A workshop about "everything" will always end up wishy-washy and vague.

If you find yourself facing a wildly varied audience, then you'll need to search for the unifying thread which ties them all together. For example, do they share a common challenge, goal, worldview, or problem which unites them? If so, pull on that thread until you find a few important insights, takeaways, skills, or tools which will be high-impact for most everyone there.

If there's simply zero overlap between the groups, then you're in an admittedly tough spot. The best option is to outmaneuver the whole issue in advance through proactively announcing who the event is *not* for. If you must teach everyone (for example, in corporate training), then you can try splitting the group into multiple separate sessions. If that's not viable, then you'll sometimes just be forced to choose one subgroup of the audience to serve while ignoring everyone else.

Gathering an Audience Profile is simple, but important. It's not something you outgrow. I still ask the organizer for this sort of info for every workshop I run. And when I mess it up, my workshops suffer, as we saw in Moscow.[7] Don't design blind; start with who's in the room.

> **Workshop design task (2-5 minutes):** Write down your Audience Profile. If you aren't sure who is likely to be in the room, send an email to the event organizer or host asking them to clarify.

Add the breaks before designing the content

Coffee breaks tend to get treated like second-class citizens in the world of workshop design. But if your workshop is longer than about 90 minutes, then the breaks are really, really important.

In fact, nothing will maintain your audience's energy as effectively as just inserting an ample break (i.e. 15 minutes for coffee, 60 minutes for lunch) after every 60-90 minutes of content. Sounds simple, and it is. But you'd be shocked at how often facilitators scrimp on their breaks in order to bludgeon the audience with Just One More Thing.

Pre-allocating your breaks ensures that you never create a toxic schedule with insufficient time for rest. It also simplifies the design challenge by dividing one big stretch of time into several little ones, each of which can be attacked independently. Plus, the existence of these small "schedule chunks" forces you to define precisely

---

[7] As a sort of playful vengeance for my less-than-stellar performance, my hosts later took me out to a bar and ordered me a dinner of lightly-fried brain with a side of brain pâté (and some bread, thankfully).

how much time you intend to spend on each Learning Outcome, which prevents you from ending up with a lopsided, awkward schedule and feeling like you're rushing to get through everything.

Here's the good news: chunking a schedule is ridiculously easy. There's usually a clear "best" way to divide up any particular block of time. And while you might adjust it a bit to account for something like an unusual lunch time, there's nothing overly mysterious at work. Here are a few examples:

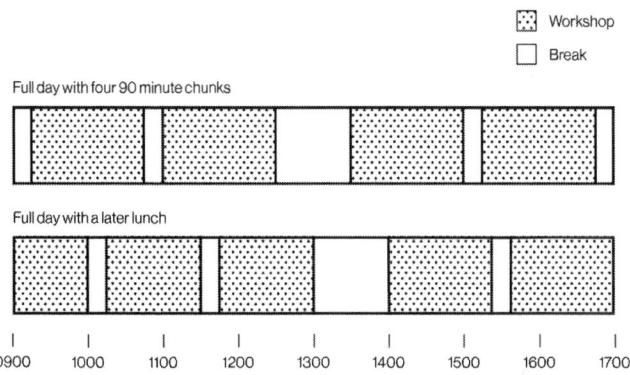

Seen above, a full day (eight hours) divides beautifully into four chunks of 90 minutes, plus two coffee breaks, an hour for lunch, and 15 minutes on either end for folks to arrive and mingle. One downside is that an early start can lead to a strangely early lunch (0900 start means lunch at 1230). One way to delay the lunch would be to use three (much shorter) chunks in the morning, followed by two (slightly shorter) chunks in the afternoon. The second example has also done away with the buffer time at the beginning and end, although that isn't strictly necessary.

A half day (four hours) works easily as either two or three chunks:

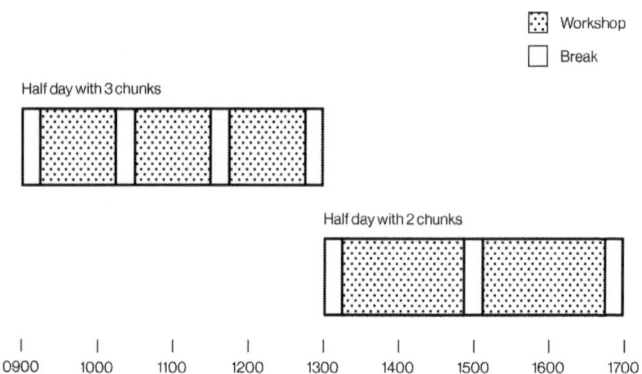

Four hours can also accommodate a lunch break by using two chunks and sacrificing some of the padding on the ends.

A three-hour workshop fits well as two 75-minute chunks, plus a 15-minute break and an extra 15 minutes at either start or end for arrivals or networking. And a two-hour workshop will usually be a single chunk, plus some optional padding:

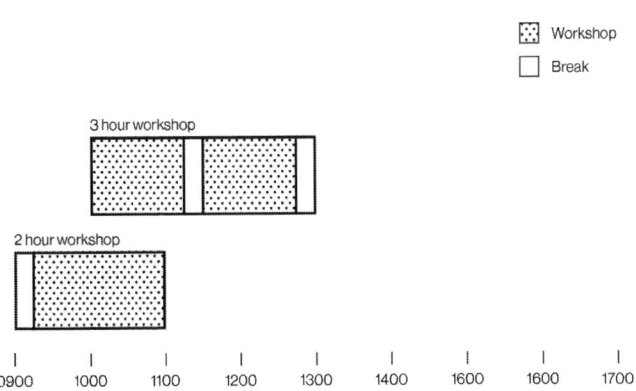

While the question of starting late will depend largely on cultural expectations, secretly planning for an early ending is always a good idea if the workshop is longer than a couple hours. The benefits are numerous: a buffer for slipped schedules, an extra opportunity for Q&A or networking, time for beer, or allowing for individual work on homework tasks or feedback forms. Plus, people *hate* running late, whereas nobody in history has ever been upset about ending 15 minutes early.

Schedule Chunks aren't set in stone and can be adjusted as you start developing your content; the main point of figuring them out first is simply to ensure that you never inadvertently create a day with a toxic schedule and that your attendees always get their breaks.

Coffee breaks are sacred. It's a big blunder to skip (or even just reduce) a break in order to cram in more stuff. In one fell swoop, the break-skipping facilitator manages to damage energy levels, violate the schedule, and diminish the audience's ability to pay attention. Unforgivable!

> **Workshop design task (2-5 minutes):** Create your Schedule Chunks by adding your breaks. Draw out your total available time, decide on whether to use an intro/outro buffer, place your breaks, and figure out how much time you have for teaching.

Sharpen your Learning Outcomes

There's a right and a wrong way to define your Learning Outcomes. And doing it right is surprisingly tough, since making them specific enough tends to feel like you're leaving stuff out. But in order to succeed at teaching *something*, you must be willing to exclude everything else.

Your first pass at your Learning Outcomes will always be too vague. Resist the urge to settle at this point. You are not a Wikipedia article; it's not your job to summarize an entire subject. Instead, your job is to provide your audience with a small, curated set of sharp, useful takeaways which meaningfully improve their lives. A workshop designer is a curator and deciding what's *out* is as important as deciding what is *in*.

Here's what I mean:

Broad Topic	Bad Learning Outcomes (too vague)	Sharp Learning Outcomes
Sales	Negotiation	How to de-escalate a tense negotiation when you're in too deep
	Proposals	The three requirements of every great sales proposal
Weddings	Decorations	The most beautiful (and cheapest!) solution to the flower problem
	Planning	How to build a budget spreadsheet to save dozens of hours of frustration and fighting
Careers	CVs (resumes)	What to delete from your CV to make it stronger
	Interviews	The right answers to the toughest interview questions

A bad Learning Outcome is a too-vague topic. As a designer, it offers no help in deciding what to include and what to cut. The clearer you can be at this stage, the simpler everything else becomes.

I was recently helping a friend prepare for his first full-day workshop (about enterprise sales). He started asking questions about tactical stuff like facilitation and exercises and group work, so I interrupted:

> *"Who is in the audience? Why have they shown up? What are they hoping to learn?"*

He knew his audience well, which was great, so I continued probing:

> *"Okay. Your workshop is about 'sales'... But what's the specific argument you're making? What are you really trying to convince them of? What do they believe differently at the end of your session compared to when they first walked in?"*

He thought for a moment and replied:

> *"That 'good sales' isn't about your pitch or presentation or banter, but is really about asking good questions."*

Boom. There's his sharp Learning Outcome: "Good sales is about asking good questions". After going through the same process for the rest of his talking points, he soon had a short list of clear, concrete takeaways. **Now that he knew what his workshop was actually about, he was able to tear through his deck, deleting everything which didn't directly support his Learning Outcomes and strengthening the bits that did.** Following his workshop, he mentioned that it had felt more "organized", which made it easier to prepare for, easier to keep on schedule, and easier for his participants to understand. That's all true. Once you've got good Learning Outcomes, everything else gets easier.

Alright. So how many Learning Outcomes can you fit into your workshop? The annoyingly vague (but honest) response is that it depends on how long you'll need to properly teach each of them. The more concrete (but less true) suggestion is to start with a guess of 30-45 minutes per Learning Outcome, and then modify it as needed.

Thirty minutes might feel like too much time to spend on one (big) idea, but it actually vanishes rather quickly. For example: 10 minutes of introductory lecture, 10 minutes of some sort of exercise and discussion, 5 minutes of follow-up lecture, and 5 minutes of Q&A. That's your half hour gone. And if you're hoping to run more than a single exercise, then you're almost certainly going to be brushing up closer to 45 minutes than to 30.

This guideline means that a 90-minute chunk can fit 2-3 Learning Outcomes, which gives you 3ish big takeaways in a 90-minute session, 6ish in a half day, and up to 12 in a full-day. That being said, my personal preference with longer workshops is to spend more time per Learning Outcome as opposed to trying to squeeze in more of them.

> **Workshop design task** (5 minutes): Take a first guess at how many major Learning Outcomes will fit in your available time, and then write out a list of them. If you end up too many or too few, that's okay for now.

> **Workshop design task** (10-15 minutes): Go through your list of Learning Outcomes and try to sharpen them as much as possible. Ask yourself whether this a clear, meaningful takeaway for the people in the room, or just a description of a too-vague "topic".

Each Learning Outcome is a cluster of related ideas

The exact size and scope of a Learning Outcome is a bit slippery to pin down. You can think of it as a cluster of closely-related ideas, each of which needs to be worked through and taught before the main takeaway can fully click into place. Or you can think of the Learning Outcome as the thesis for a high school essay, which needs to be built up to and delivered through a handful of supporting or key ideas or building blocks. These talking points are the mini-takeaways on your path toward the big one.

The crucial question when figuring out these sub-points is:

> *"What else do they need to know, believe, or be able to do in order for them to properly absorb the main Learning Outcome?"*

As before, you'll likely have more ideas than will fit in your workshop. And as before, it's about both curation (picking the highest-impact few) and sharpness (honing them until they offer a concrete lesson-learned).

Here's an example of a full outline for a workshop on weddings. It has three Learning Outcomes, each of which has been expanded out into a small cluster of closely related ideas:

```
"Stress-Free Wedding Planning"

1. The budget spreadsheet is your new
best friend

    -   The most common ways weddings go
        over budget
    -   Fixed expenses (venue, dress) vs.
        per-guest expenses (food, booze)
    -   How to use your spreadsheet as a
        project management super-tool

2. Turn your big day into a no-stress
checklist

    -   How the humble checklist keeps hos-
        pitals running
    -   The challenge with weddings: too
        many cooks in the kitchen
    -   How to create and use your three
        crucial checklists

3. How to delegate without going crazy

    -   The trouble with "free" help from
        family and friends
    -   How to keep an eye on everything
        without turning into a microman-
        ager
```

This outline shows what your workshop is *really* about. Not a vague topic, but a set of clear takeaways.

It's quick to create, quick to iterate, and hugely simplifies the task of delivering a wonderful workshop.

When you eventually start making your slides (not yet!), you can follow the outline to create a deck which is laser-focused on exactly what you're trying to say. This helps avoid rambling, keeps you on schedule, and ensures a session where the attendees actually learn something.

Although it usually only takes about an hour to get through all the steps up to this point, it can be wise to pause here and let it simmer in your mind for a few days, if you have the time. It's a bus-stop task: when you're stuck waiting somewhere, you take out your workshop outline instead of your phone.

Another purpose of the pause is to gather feedback from a client, organizer, or potential audience-member. This moment *right now* is the highest-impact for getting feedback. The outline provides enough detail that folks can understand exactly what you're going to be teaching, and you haven't done any "extra" work (like slides) that would need to be discarded in case of major changes. Nobody bothers to do this, which is ludicrous. It's an easy email to write:

The Workshop Survival Guide

Hello Jackie, I know you're starting to think about your wedding and hoped you might give me some feedback on a workshop I'm putting together, called "Stress-Free Wedding Planning".

The outline is below. Do any topics jump out as something you'd really like to learn? Do any seem boring or irrelevant? And is anything missing? Thanks!

"Stress-Free Wedding Planning"

1. The budget spreadsheet is your new best friend

- ...[Full workshop outline continues]...

```
Hey Beth, I'm already stressing like
crazy, so sounds like something I
need. Although I've got to say, I'm
not so keen about poking around in
spreadsheets for half the time. I get
enough of that at my job.

Also, something I'd love to hear about
is what to do when something goes
wrong... Like the flowers get lost or
you forget your dress at home.⁸ I know
you'll probably say I don't need to
worry about what hasn't happened, but
I do, and I think I'd feel a lot better
if I knew how to handle even the rare
disasters.
```

If there's nobody to get feedback from (or you're doing everything last-minute and don't have time to ask), then you'll just have to use your best guess. After you've run the workshop the first time, you'll spot opportunities for improvement and can tweak it from there.

Even if you don't make meaningful changes to the content itself, this sort of feedback is still invaluable for finding the words and descriptions which most resonate with your attendees.

Once you've got the outline, you can use it verbatim as part of your marketing and promotional material. (If you're marketing your own events, this also

---

[8] This was the plot twist of Devin's wedding, leading to an all-night recovery mission and a sleep-deprived groom. But all ended well, with much jubilation and peacocks everywhere.

means you can start selling tickets at this point; if nobody buys any, then you know you need to fix something.)

Some facilitators flinch away from being so specific in their event blurbs, because they don't want to "exclude" anyone. But it's much better for folks to know precisely what you're going to be covering, which allows them to decide whether your workshop is going to be relevant for them. When you promote too vaguely, you end up with a bunch of people in the room who don't actually want to learn what you're teaching.

> **Workshop design** task (5-10 minutes): Create a full workshop outline by expanding your Learning Outcomes into a cluster of supporting arguments or key ideas.

> **Workshop design task** (2 minutes, plus some waiting): Send your workshop outline to a client or potential attendee for feedback.

Workshop Outline + Schedule Chunks = Workshop Skeleton

At this stage in the design process, you should be holding three main building blocks for your soon-to-be workshop:

1. An **Audience Profile** (which has already done its job of informing your Learning Outcomes, and can thus be set aside for now)
2. A **set of Schedule Chunks** (which you got by inserting generous coffee and lunch breaks into your allotted time)
3. An **outline of Learning Outcomes and supporting arguments** (a simple list on a scrap of paper is fine)

We're now going to do some complicated science by smooshing together the outline and the schedule. Let's review what we're working with and build it up into a completed Skeleton. To start with, we've got our Workshop Outline:

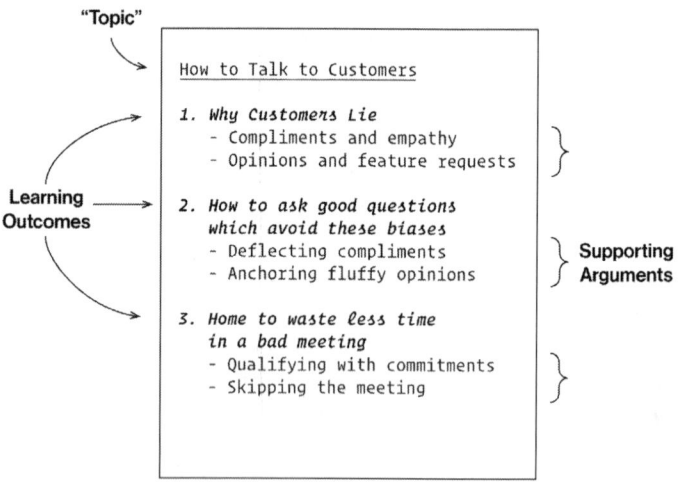

No surprises so far. Then we've got our schedule. I like to draw it out as a little timeline. Here's an example of a three-hour session:

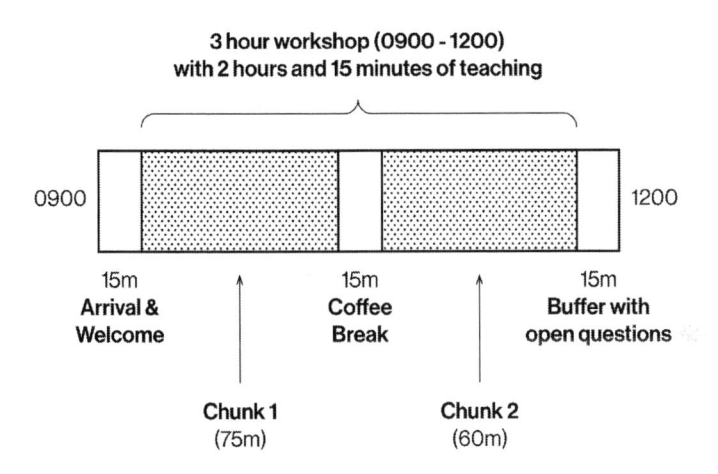

```
        3 hour workshop (0900 - 1200)
        with 2 hours and 15 minutes of teaching

0900  ┌──┬──────────┬──┬─────────┬──┐  1200
      │  │░░░░░░░░░░│  │░░░░░░░░░│  │
      └──┴──────────┴──┴─────────┴──┘
       15m            15m           15m
    Arrival &        Coffee       Buffer with
    Welcome          Break       open questions

             Chunk 1         Chunk 2
             (75m)           (60m)
```

You'll see that in this case, I've chosen to include 15 minutes on each end for arrival, departure, and as a time buffer, which uses 30 minutes. And including a break reduces our "3-hour workshop" down to 2 hours and 15 minutes of actual teaching time. But you could also easily decide that the introductory time isn't needed, expanding the content to 2h 30m. (Incidentally, failing to allow time for these sorts of predictable delays is the reason certain facilitators seem to run late every single time they teach.)

Now we smoosh it together. Before getting fancy, I recommend the time-tested approach of just blindly jamming your Learning Outcomes into whatever schedule you've come up with. It doesn't *always* work, but it works more often than you'd expect. So it might look something like this:

```
     ①                    ③
Why customers lie    How to waste less time
    (45m)                 (45m)
```

```
                    ②
            Asking good questions
                   (45m)
```

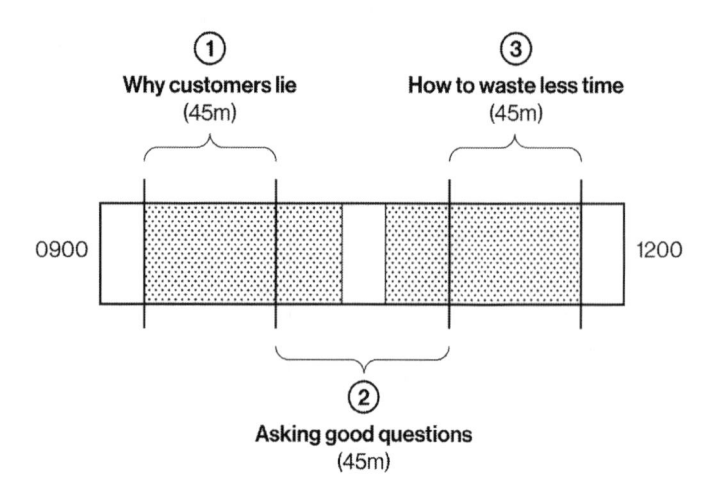

In this example, my 2h 15m (135 minutes) of content are divided between three Learning Outcomes. This allows 45 minutes for each major takeaway, which is extremely comfortable.

Having extra time is rarely a problem: just run more exercises or take more questions. But having too little time (and too many Learning Outcomes) very well might be. **So we pause at this point to take a quick look and see if it passes a sanity check. Does it seem roughly plausible? Or are we trying to teach something too complex in too little time?** If it feels crammed, then we'll need to free up some time from somewhere, which usually means cutting something. This is a hard choice, but it's best to do it now. If you ignore the squeeze, then it's still going to hit you, except it will do so on the day-of when it's too late to fix. And then you'll feel rushed, talk fast, compromise the breaks, drain the energy, snap the goodwill, run late anyway, and generally make everyone sad.

We don't yet know any of the specifics of our exercises. But that's okay! Our goal for now is to build is a set of guidelines and constraints which will keep us on track when we eventually *are* dealing with those details. Three hours of blank space is a scary and difficult thing to fill; 45 minutes (or whatever) to figure out how to teach "Why they lie" is far more doable.

I like using the visual timeline to see the overall shape of the session, and then add timings to my outline to get a (mostly) finished Workshop Skeleton:

How to Talk to Customers

[0900-0915] *Arrival, coffee, mingling, and welcome*

[0915-1000] *Why customers lie*
   a. Compliments and empathy
   b. Opinions and feature requests

[1000-1100] *How to ask good questions which
                 avoid these biases*
   a. Deflecting compliments
   b. [1030-1045] << *Coffee break* >>
   c. Anchoring fluffy opinions

[1100-1145] *How to waste less time in bad meetings*
   a. Qualifying with commitments
   b. Skipping the meeting

[1145-1200] *Wrap-up, questions, & schedule buffer*

Super simple, super helpful. It provides the constraints that allow you to be creative without going crazy. Later in the design process, we'll improve this Skeleton by adding exercises and activities. It's our guiding light for the rest of the design process.

The Skeleton also helps during facilitation. Whenever I run a workshop, I keep a folded sheet of paper in my pocket with the Skeleton written on it. As I finish each section, I take a quick look and mentally (or literally) tick off its Learning Outcome(s). This reminds me to cover everything, and also offers early warning if I'm starting to run late. Great! (Incidentally, much of becoming a better facilitator isn't actually about getting "better", but rather about doing stuff ahead of time which makes your life easier on the day-of.)

Next up: picking your exercises and improving the workshop's energy levels.

> **Workshop Design Task** (5-10 minutes): Create a Workshop Skeleton by inserting your Learning Outcomes into your Schedule Chunks.

> **Workshop Design Task** (5-10 minutes): Do a quick sanity check on the Skeleton. Does it seem plausible to teach those ideas in those amounts of time? If your content doesn't seem to fit at all, try adjusting either the Learning Outcomes or schedule chunks. Or try reordering to see how that might affect the flow. If it's still too crowded, you probably need to cut something.

Lessons learned:

- Workshop Outline + Schedule Chunks = Workshop Skeleton
- Creating a good Skeleton is the single most important step in designing an effective, high-energy workshop and should be completed *before* getting into slide design

Vary the Teaching Formats to improve energy, attention, and learning

Teaching Formats are the "genres" of teaching. They're what you use to actually deliver your content. They define the feel and structure of your exercises. You already know a bunch of them: lecture, small group discussion, Q&A, and so on.

But even for the familiar-sounding Formats, folks still tend to misunderstand how and when to use them. Before getting into the details of each, here are two overarching principles:

- The Teaching Format should "match" whatever you're currently teaching
- The Teaching Format should switch at least every 20 minutes

There are a couple reasons for these rules. First and foremost, different types of lessons are best delivered through different styles of teaching. To play off the example from the intro, let's say you were defying common sense and attempting to "teach yoga with a lecture". Furthermore, let's imagine that it wasn't going terribly well, and that your students weren't improving as much as you would like. The solution, in this case, would *not* be to deliver a better lecture. No matter how brilliant your story-telling or how charismatic your delivery, a lecture is simply the wrong tool for the job. Yoga is a hands-on skill, so you'd need to teach it with some sort of hands-on practice (as opposed to with a knowledge-heavy lecture). That's the "matching" of a Teaching Format to a topic, and it goes a long way toward ensuring that folks can successfully learn from you.

The second rule—to regularly switch between different Formats—is partly because the variation boosts energy levels and attention, and partly to force you outside of your teaching comfort zone. Each of us has a "comfort Format" (usually lecture) which we overuse by default, despite secretly knowing that a better option might exist if only we spent the time and effort to search for it. So a big benefit of the "you must mix it up" rule is simply in forcing yourself to stare at a blank page for long enough to invent something non-obvious.

When I was little, I remember sitting on the countertop while the kettle was boiling. As the steam began to swirl and whistle, I assumed it was some sort of refreshing mist and crawled in that direction, intent on sticking my face in it. My dad caught hold of me just in time, and while I'm sure he was tempted to react with an enthusiastically-delivered lecture, I'm equally sure that I would have completely failed to learn from it. But instead, he cobbled together a sort of impromptu workshop, complete with a variety of Teaching Formats.

He seemed to want to teach me that a) heat can hurt and b) things can be hot even when they don't *look* hot, so c) there are certain things that you should always be cautious about getting close to. We began by using a thermometer to measure the temperature of the tap water as it heated up. We felt it by hand, and also wrote down the numbers from the thermometer up until the point where I said it was "really hot" (say 40°C) and took my hand away. We continued by measuring the temperature of a pan of boiling water ("so much hotter!"), running a little experiment to prove that hot water *becomes* steam, and discussing the implications. In the end, I resolved never to go near the kettle again, and—once I was old enough to make these sorts of decisions for myself—to refrain from casually storing a thermonuclear device on my kitchen counter.

Throughout this little "workshop", dad used three different Teaching Formats: hands-on experiments, pair discussions, and brief bits of lecture to string it all together and deliver missing theoretical concepts. Each activity was well-suited to the takeaway under discussion, and they worked cohesively to build toward the primary Learning Outcome. And since he repeatedly switched between different types of activities, it was easy for me—even as a hyperactive young child—to stay focused on the task at hand.

And more importantly, I actually *learned*. While you, as a teacher, will never be able to unilaterally cram knowledge into an unwilling student's head, you certainly *can* design your workshop in a way which creates the right conditions for them to more easily pay attention and, hopefully, to learn.

Variation between Formats acts to refresh attention and energy. And conversely, staying with the same Teaching Format for too long will eventually start to drain the audience, no matter how "high energy" that particular exercise appears on its own. This phenomenon is called Format Fatigue and can help explain why something that worked brilliantly for 15 minutes can start feeling like a real drag at 30.

When new facilitators notice their audience nodding off, they'll often try to fix it by cranking up their own performance as a teacher. This doesn't work. Dancing around the stage like a wide-eyed lunatic may prove that you care, but your enthusiasm still can't cross the air gap. What your students actually *experience* is the workshop's underlying design, and that's where you must work to influence their energy and attention. It doesn't require any fancy facilitation or grand performance. Once you know the "trick", maintaining strong energy across a long workshop is laughably simple: all it requires is good breaks and variation between Teaching Formats.

But what if you're facing three back-to-back sections which are each begging to be taught with the same Format? Should you accept the penalty of Format Fatigue, or should you switch one of them to a suboptimal Format? This turns out to be a false dichotomy. Much better, instead, to either swap the order of your existing sections (AAABB → ABABA) or to create and insert some small new exercises in the middle, just to keep everyone feeling fresh (AAA → ACADA). Or, if it's a long enough workshop to have a coffee break, you can sometimes jiggle the schedule such that the break falls right in the middle of the too-long section. Any of these options will prevent Format Fatigue, boost energy, and refresh attention. (Incidentally, this is a perfect example of how workshop *design* — rather than facilitation — creates strong energy levels.)

Format changes don't need to be big to be effective. For example, you could switch from working in small groups to working in pairs. Although both "group work", the shifting team dynamics will be enough to partially refresh your audience. Similarly, the switches don't need to be lengthy. If you have a long and unavoidable lecture, for example, then you might choose to interrupt it every 15 minutes for a quick, five-minute micro exercise.

Lesson learned:

- To avoid "teaching yoga with a lecture", pick a Teaching Format which matches the nature of what you're currently trying to teach
- To maintain attention and energy, switch Teaching Format at least every 20 minutes

The five essential Teaching Formats

So, what are your Teaching Format options?

Although there are plenty of specialized options for difficult and unusual situations (which are detailed in the Appendix), the five essential Formats covered here will be used in pretty much every workshop you ever design. And furthermore, they are sufficient—all on their own—to design and run a brilliant workshop on almost any topic.

As mentioned, you'll already be broadly familiar with the essential Formats. Still, I'd encourage you to read through the upcoming sections anyway. The magic is often in the details and folks tend to get these "simple" Formats more wrong than right.

The five essential Teaching Formats are:

- **Lectures** (for delivering "book knowledge" and extracting takeaways from exercises)
- **Small group and pair discussions** (for wrestling with ambiguous options and personal implications)
- **"Try it now"** practice (for building hands-on skills)

- **Scenario challenges** (for building wisdom, evaluation, judgement, and decision-making)
- **Question & answer** (for catching major objections/confusion and adding some flexibility into your schedule)

These formats are easy to design around, simple to facilitate, and can be used to teach a brilliant workshop of any duration about practically any subject. Each has its own strengths and constraints which you must understand to properly wield it.

Format 1: Lectures have their place

During any workshop, there will be times when you need everyone to stop talking, pay attention, and listen to you deliver some crucial piece of knowledge. These are your lecture segments. They'll typically last for 5-20 minutes and be tightly focused on delivering some knowledge-heavy piece of a Learning Outcome. A typical workshop will include several different lecture segments, arranged such that they alternate with more engaging types of exercises.

Lectures are the scapegoat of the workshop world. It's common to hear an event organizer say, "We want a fun, interactive workshop, not a *boring lecture*." And while I agree that lectures do tend to be overused and misapplied, they're invaluable when applied properly toward what they're good at.

In the context of a workshop, lectures are good for:

1. Delivering "pure" book knowledge, theory, examples, and stories
2. Supporting an upcoming exercise by establishing the theoretical foundations

3. Supporting a just-finished exercise by extracting and discussing the lessons-learned and takeaways

Lectures become bad when they overstay their welcome, running uninterrupted for too long (i.e. more than 15-20 minutes) and when they attempt to teach topics and takeaways for which they are poorly-suited. If you have a tendency toward lecture, then here's a rule of thumb to greatly improve your workshops:

Every piece of lecture should be paired with an exercise which attacks the same topic from a more interactive direction.

For example: First you do a bit of lecture, and then you run a small group discussion about its implications. Then a bit more lecture, and then a dose of hands-on "try it now" practice. A bit more lecture, and then a scenario challenge focused on evaluation and decision-making. This approach allows you to continue using lecture segments as the core vehicle of knowledge delivery, while also ensuring that you've built a lively, interesting, and effective workshop.

For more practical topics, you can just as easily reverse this pattern, treating the *other* Teaching Formats as the core of your workshop, and then occasionally including a touch of lecture to add the theory, anecdotes, or examples. After all, even the most hands-on skills still depend on at least a little bit of theory. For example, if you were teaching a pottery workshop, you might find yourself interrupting the hands-on practice to deliver a short lecture explaining the trade-offs of the various types of clays and glazes. And an hour of hands-on yoga could easily include a few minutes of "lecture" on the safety considerations of a certain posture.

So, if workshop lectures *can* be good, then why are most of them so bad? Even if you're using a lecture in the right place and for the right purpose, it's still possible to fail in its execution. I think this happens largely because folks lose sight of their Learning Outcomes and end up waffling along on tangents (and then wondering how they've run late yet again).

Some time ago, on a trip through Romania, I attended a lecture-heavy workshop featuring lovely slides, a charismatic speaker, and a compelling metaphor of strategy-as-dance. The facilitator clearly held the knowledge I wanted to learn, proven by the fact that she was continually sharing fascinating examples and case studies. But I couldn't figure out how they fit together into a lesson I could take away. In other words, she had topics, but no Learning Outcomes.[9] In any case, despite paying full attention and taking diligent notes, I left her session with zero understanding of what I was supposed to have taken away.

Folks with deep expertise are especially vulnerable to the tangent trap, since they know a ton of stuff and are highly tempted to include it all. But that's how you end up with a rambly, vague lecture. Instead, start with the main Learning Outcomes, add a few key supporting arguments, and delete anything which doesn't directly support those points. (This should sound familiar… It's Workshop Skeletons 101.)

You may think that this reduction leads to an empty, vapid lecture, but it's really quite the opposite. Most speakers greatly underestimate how much time

---

[9] Or she arguably had the one Learning Outcome of "strategy is like a dance" but failed to build up to it with a coherent set of supporting arguments and exercises. Even if that *was* her Learning Outcome, it still might have benefitted from being sharpened into a more concrete takeaway.

an audience requires to absorb and digest what's being said. Even the great Sir Ken Robinson, orator of TED's most-viewed presentation of all time, limits himself to three main points per 20-minute talk. And rather than obsessing over the exact details of every slide and sentence, he says that the bulk of his preparation involves nothing more than a short outline of key takeaways. Here's his description of his process:[10]

> *"I hadn't written the speech out, I hadn't rehearsed it, I hadn't practiced it, and I certainly hadn't memorized it. But what I had is the arc of the talk I wanted to give.*
>
> *I always think of it in five pieces, truthfully. It's bookended by an intro and a conclusion, and there's a three-part section in the middle with a set of premises I want to deal with. I kind of develop them and then I wrap it up.*
>
> *I have some notes in my pocket with just some bullet points. It's like a set list, is how I think of it, because every audience is different, and every occasion is different."*

As far as I can reckon, Sir Ken's three-part middle isn't so different from a Learning Outcome's cluster of closely related ideas. And there is also a certain similarity between your Workshop Skeleton and Sir Ken's "set list". There's something to be said for creating enough guidance to keep you on-track, without becoming so detail-obsessed that you limit your ability to deliver something tailored to the folks in the room.

---

[10] Excerpted from the TED podcast, with minor edits to word ordering for clarity. The full interview is at:
https://www.ted.com/talks/sir_ken_robinson_sir_ken robinson_still_wants_an_education_revolution

A vicious cycle exists between lengthy (and thus draining) lectures and trying to include too much stuff in your workshop. From the teacher's perspective, lectures *feel* like the fastest way to "get through" something. So if you've flinched away from making tough cuts when designing your Skeleton, it's tempting to start dropping exercises and turning everything into a lecture to "get through" it all.

But even if you can manage, this apparent success is an educational illusion: although your lecture has *told* the audience what they are supposed to have learned, there is absolutely zero guarantee that anybody has actually *learned* any of it. Worse still, by zipping ahead to "get through" the next topic, you won't even realize how lost the students have become.

The crucial takeaway? Use lecture in small doses for what it's good at, constrained by well-defined Learning Outcomes and complemented by exercises built from the other, more interactive Teaching Formats. Speaking of which…

Format 2: Small group & pair discussions

Let's go out on a limb here: small group discussion is the ultimate Teaching Format. When used properly it's engaging, inclusive, widely applicable, encourages debate, is easy to run, and lets the attendees get to know each other in an educational and non-awkward way. If you get good enough at designing and running discussions, you'll be able to successfully create workshops of any duration about pretty much any topic. It also requires no equipment or fancy room setup. It's so easy and so reliable that it nearly feels like cheating.

That being said, almost everybody screws it up. This can happen on the facilitation-side thanks to slow

The Workshop Survival Guide

and high-friction group formation (which we'll return to in Part 2). But the biggest mistakes tend to be committed earlier, during the design stage, in the form of weak prompts for what to talk about.

Asking your students to, "Turn to your neighbor and discuss" seems harmless but is actually impossibly vague. Nine times out of ten, someone in each group will tentatively ask something like:

"So, what did you think?"

And their partner(s) will respond with:

"Well, it seems pretty interesting. What did you think?"

At this point, the conversation is already dead, your exercise has failed, and your workshop has worsened. The students will sit in awkward silence for about 30 seconds and then start either talking about their personal lives or turning to their phones. This one lazy discussion prompt has now damaged your energy levels, reduced your goodwill, and has *also* failed in its goal of supporting your Learning Outcomes. Not good.

Instead, you need to instruct your participants—explicitly and specifically—what they're supposed to be talking about. And just saying it out loud isn't enough, because they'll inevitably forget and go off track. You need to write it somewhere visible (usually a slide) and leave it there for the duration of the exercise.

Prompts don't need to be complicated to be good. For example, here's a perfectly sufficient prompt for a discussion about entrepreneurial career paths:

> Starting a company sucks.
>
> Why bother doing it?

Good prompts allow for good conversations, and it's your job to figure them out, in advance, and ensure that they're clear, interesting, and relevant.

Now, although the discussion's *question* should be clear and specific, its *answer* should be ambiguous and/or personal. Small group discussion is at its strongest when folks are wrestling with—and hearing multiple perspectives on—tough issues with no factual "right" answer. For example, there's not much value in doing a group discussion about something factual, like the legal implications of certain types of business funding. But there's a lot of value in having folks discuss which type of funding they think would be right *for them*, and why. Make the question sharp, but its answer personal.

Let's say you're running a career planning workshop for graduating high school seniors. Some of your students have been primed (by their family, friends, and pop culture) to choose the career with the highest status and/or salary, so they all want to be bankers and lawyers. Others have been primed (by those same forces) to prioritize purpose, so *they* all want to be artists and dolphin trainers. There's no "right" answer to the question of which path to pick, or even of how to evaluate the available options. But there certainly might be value in mixing up those two types of people and having them wrestle with some meaty questions about, for example, lifestyle goals and monthly budgets and where else they might find both purpose and pleasure. Group discussion allows them to reflect on those questions, while also hearing fresh perspectives on the same.

Of course, the prompt still needs to relate to and support your Learning Outcomes. Your attendees will smell trickery if you're having them talk about pointless stuff. But pretty much every Learning Outcome will have some sort of opportunity for discussion and reflection. Even for something impossibly dry (like talking about safe driving at traffic school), you can usually still find a good discussion prompt with a bit of creative effort (like asking folks to share the story of when another driver made them most frightened on the road).

In terms of scheduling, the discussions themselves should be fairly brief (2-5 minutes), but the overall exercise will still end up consuming a decent chunk of your schedule (10-15 minutes).

Where do those extra minutes go? The first minute might go into ensuring that everyone has a group and that nobody is stranded. (Always finish group formation before showing them the prompt.) If this is the first time these particular groups have worked together, then you may (optionally) carve out 2-3 minutes for them to say hello and get to know each other. Once everyone is settled, the next minute is spent explaining the discussion prompt, followed by the 2-5 minutes for the small group discussion itself. Taken together, this all puts you at the 5-10 minute mark. After the task, you'll want to run a class-wide discussion, asking a couple participants to share their takeaways, spreading the learning while also allowing you to chime in with your own perspective. These post-exercise discussions can be wonderfully high-value and will easily fill 5-10 minutes without feeling like a drag. (We'll talk about how to smoothly facilitate this step in Part 2.) And that's your 15 minutes up and gone.

If you feel that the discussion topic is so large that folks will need more than five minutes to get into it, then it's probably too vague and should be broken into pieces. Attendees tend to get wildly off-track if they're given too much time on any one task, so you should strongly consider subdividing large discussions into several smaller, more time-constrained prompts, run one after the other.

Using pairs instead of groups offers a slightly different set of benefits. Small groups have the advantage of multiple perspectives, with the downside that some attendees might choose to zone out and become a passive observer throughout the exercise. Pairs, on the other hand, have the advantage of forcing everyone to participate, but with less exposure to multiple ideas. This makes *groups* better for exposing folks to new perspectives, whereas *pairs* are better for tasks where you want attendees—all of them—to work through a problem or come up with an idea.

Small group and pair discussions are game changing. Use them! As long as you've spent the time to design good prompts (clear question, ambiguous answer), I promise it will work wonders.

> **Workshop Design Task:** For each of your Learning Outcomes or key ideas, try to come up with at least one good discussion prompt. You don't necessarily need to use all of them, but it's useful practice to force yourself to identify the ambiguous, personal side of what you're teaching, even for topics which don't seem to be an obvious fit.

Format 3: Q&A is for flexibility, not interactivity

You should add a bit of Q&A (question & answer) to pretty much every workshop. But perhaps not for the reason you think.

Unstructured Q&A is a bad educational format. Even when used properly, Q&A suffers from an irredeemable flaw: the least confident students will never speak up. This is less of a problem if you're teaching people with universally robust egos, like executives. But when trying to educate regular people, Q&A abandons those who need you most.

While that one issue is more than enough to condemn Q&A, it also tends to *hurt* energy levels rather than to help them, since the pace is slow and it's not actually interactive for anyone except the one person currently asking the question. Plus, students can easily hijack Q&A (either accidentally or maliciously) to self-promote and showboat. And all these problems only get worse as the audience gets larger.

Q&A's most gratuitous abuse is as a way to pretend that a long, dreary lecture is actually a fun, "interactive" discussion. This is extremely common and is clearly just a coverup for a speaker who forgot to design an actual workshop.

So, Q&A has problems. But you should still include it. And there are good reasons for that.

The most self-evident benefit of Q&A is that it allows the crowd to catch you if your teaching has missed the mark by such a grand degree that nobody in the audience has any idea what you're talking about. While you can never count on a confused *individual* to speak up, you can always count on somebody within a confused *class* to do so. In this latter case, the confident students can speak up on behalf of everyone else to let you know that you're going to need to loop back and clarify. This is obviously a reassuring safety net, especially when dealing with a new topic or audience. But that's not the *main* reason to include it.

Q&A's primary purpose is to be deleted when you're running late. This Format's greatest value lies in the fact that it is a credible—but not essential—way to fill an ambiguous amount of time. And it's flexible. You can easily shrink a section of Q&A to five minutes or lengthen it to 20 without anyone knowing that you're deviating from the plan. This sort of flexibility is *extremely* helpful for staying on schedule and ending on time.

Most of a workshop's schedule is fairly rigid, which means there's no way to recover from schedule slippage without deleting something important. So you include Q&A as a flexible "schedule spring" which can stretch and shrink to soak up changes in the timing elsewhere. The inclusion of these springs is *the* secret to finishing exactly on time, even if you're starting late or running behind. You'll never be able to recover time by just talking faster; instead, you need to design some flex into your schedule. Springs are a useful general design concept, and I recommend including at least 15 minutes of spring in every 90-minute chunk of your schedule. If you're spending 30 minutes per Learning Outcome, this works out to just five minutes of Q&A per takeaway, which is fairly easy to accommodate.

Given that you're going to be using a bit of Q&A, you should make two small tweaks to help compensate for its problems:

- Instead of doing one long Q&A at the end of your workshop, do a shorter Q&A after each Learning Outcome
- Instead of vaguely asking if anyone has "any questions?", be more specific and encourage them to ask questions which are relevant to exactly what you just talked about (and include a helpful reminder about what those things are)

By breaking Q&A into small pieces pinned to each Learning Outcome, you reduce Format Fatigue and increase energy levels. And by keeping the questions tightly focused on the most recent Learning Outcomes, you improve the educational potential and make it easier to stay on topic.

Polling the class with Dot Votes and Post-Ups

I often hear teachers polling their class with a question like, "What else do you want to learn?" or "What would you like to spend more time on?" But that will only succeed in telling you what the most confident and outspoken want to learn, and it actively silences the folks who are already feeling uneasily behind. To get a representative sample of data from everyone, you need force everyone to answer by using something like a Dot Vote or Post-Up.

Dot Votes are used to let the class quickly decide between several options. Each attendee is given a fixed number of votes (usually three), which are represented physically as either a sticky note, a small sticker, or as a pen mark. The options are visibly laid out on a wall, allowing everyone to approach simultaneously to place their votes on their preferred choices. (If they really like one choice to the exclusion of the others, it's fine to spend multiple votes on one item.) I used this recently when I had an unallocated 90 minutes toward the end of a two-day workshop and wanted to ask the class what they'd like to spend it on. Here were the results:

The results of this vote were fairly even, with no obvious "winner" (although it did eliminate a few universally unwanted options). As such, I picked the top three and spent another half-hour on each, using part of my lunch break to plan the details. (I had created extra exercises for each of the six[11] main topics while designing the main workshop, so I knew I'd be prepared regardless of what was chosen.)

---

[11] You may have noticed that the voting boards in the photo have a total of 12 options, rather than the six mentioned in the text. This is because it was a train-the-trainer workshop, so each major topic could be approached from the direction of both "how to do it" and also "how to teach it".

Another good option is a Post-Up. In a Post-Up, you ask the audience a question, and everyone responds by writing something down on a sticky note. They then come forward and stick it on the wall. I sometimes do one at the very beginning of a session, just to make sure that I'm focusing on the right issues. For example, at a recent session on the mechanics of equity investment, I spent the first five minutes of the workshop by saying:

> *"I want everyone to grab a sticky note and to write down the #1 thing you're hoping to learn from this session. What's the big question that you' want to have answered? Write it down and then come up here and stick it on the wall. You don't need to wait until I call on you, just come on up whenever you're done writing."*

As a teacher, this little Post-Up has basically given me a mind-reading super-power, since I know *exactly* what I need to cover in order to make this session a huge win for everyone in the room.

Once I finished teaching and was ready to shift into Q&A, I first looked at the wall to see if I had missed anything. And of course, I had. I answered those questions first (as if an audience member had asked them to me), and then opened it up to a normal Q&A.

If you're running the Post-up at the end of a session, after you've already taught the core material, then the prompt would be more like:

> *"What were you hoping you'd learn, which we didn't have a chance to cover?"*

> *"When you go home and try to put this into practice, what are you most worried about not being able to do?"*

"Any questions? Everyone has to write down at least one, so take a minute to think through what you're still keen to hear about."

And then, as the sticky notes start appearing on the wall, just start answering them.

So, next time you're tempted to schedule 20 minutes of Q&A, try something different by spending the first few minutes of it on a quick Post-Up. (You can also use a Post-Up at the very end of a session to collect testimonials and feedback as a quicker—but less informative—alternative to a paper feedback form.)

Neither Dot Voting nor Post-Ups can fully replace unstructured Q&A. But they're certainly helpful additions which allow you to get more out of it in certain circumstances, especially when you need to know what the whole audience cares about.

Format 4: "Try it now" for practicing hands-on skills

"Try it now" is both incredibly powerful and tragically underused. The idea is simple. After introducing any concept which is even slightly skill-based, give the students a small task which allows them to immediately put it into practice in a safe, controlled environment, and under enough supportive restrictions that they can't get too far off track. Depending on your topic, this could be a major, recurring exercise within your workshop, or it could be a quick, 2-5 minute micro-exercise. Either way, participants get to try doing it, and that makes all the difference.

Some topics are so clearly skill-based that they're almost always taught via this sort of facilitated practice. For example, computer programming courses are often run with as many hours in the lab as in the lecture halls. The same holds true for music, pottery, art, sailing, sewing, writing, massage, cooking, math, medicine, and countless other hands-on disciplines. For these sorts of topics, it's easy to imagine designing a session which oscillates happily between theory and practice. For example, throughout a calligraphy workshop, you might interrupt an overarching demonstration of lettering styles (i.e. a lecture) with frequent breaks where students "try it now" by attempting to emulate a given script.

Despite its obvious virtues, this format is often overlooked when teaching theory-heavy topics. But it's crucial to remember that even the "purest" theoretical topic will still depend on a few practical sub-skills. For example, although much of an MBA can be learned from a lecture, it also depends on various hands-on tasks, such as figuring out the size of an emerging new market. And if momentum carries the teacher past this topic without stopping to do a bit of practice, then students will completely fail to learn how to actually do it. Sizing a new market depends on both knowledge *and* skill. And as such, it needs to be taught with both lecture (for the knowledge) *and* "try it now" (for the skill).

In terms of scheduling and facilitation, "try it now" is similar to small group discussion: form groups, assign a task, watch and listen to them work, and then run a class-wide discussion about what just happened. And as before, five minutes of practice can easily fill 10-15 minutes of classroom time.

Some care must be given to create a task which is neither too easy nor too hard; erring too far in either direction will prevent learning. Instead, there's a sweet spot somewhere in the middle where students can complete the task, but only with some amount of support and guidance.[12]

Thankfully, it's possible to deliver this guidance without needing to run a 1-on-1 intervention with every single participant. (Which would severely limit your audience size.) Instead, the assistance can be baked into the design of the exercise itself, guiding attendees through an otherwise undoable task and maximizing their learning in the process.

Although tasks can be "too difficult" in a variety of ways (e.g. by depending on skills that some students are missing), the most common mistake is to assign a task which actually contains several hidden sub-steps. From a students' perspective, it feels a bit like this:

---

[12] In education theory, this "sweet spot" is called the Zone of Proximal Development (ZPD).

How to draw an owl

1.   2.

1. Draw some circles   2. Draw the rest of the fucking owl

Although the example seems absurd, the mistake is incredibly common. For example, when I was helping my aforementioned friend prepare for his full-day sales workshop, one of his exercises looked like this:

> 5 minutes:
>
> **Write down the description of your perfect customer.**

While this prompt *seems* quite simple, it should set off mental alarm bells. This is exactly the sort of task which, to an expert, seems clear and easy. Whereas for a beginner, it is impossibly vague. The problem is that several steps are required in order to succeed at "describing a perfect customer". It's a multi-step prompt disguised as a single task. It's asking them to draw the owl.

And sure enough, when he had used this exercise in previous, shorter workshops, he was constantly needing to clarify and answer questions from confused students: "But what makes a good customer?" "Do you mean I should write down their age and income?" "What if I don't have any customers yet?" All these clarifications were easy for him to make. And once he had done so, participants went on to achieve good results. But the simple fact that the questions had been asked in the first place proves that his prompt was weak and vague.

You'd fix this prompt in exactly the same way you'd fix the owl tutorial: by adding clearer intermediary tasks. To figure out what those intermediary steps might be, I asked him to talk me through what he'd expect his students to consider during this exercise. He rattled off a quick list:

> *"They should think about where the customers might be physically located. And where they spend time online. Whether or not they've already tried to solve this problem and how much money they're spending on it. And... etc."*

And *this*, as you might have noticed, is precisely the series of steps a never-done-it-before attendee should go through in order to reach a good answer of who their perfect customer might be. To fix his exercise, all he needed to do was break the single big task (i.e. "draw the owl") prompt into a series of smaller ones:

> **90 seconds:**
> Where does your perfect customer hang out, both in person and online?

> **90 seconds:**
> Is your perfect customer already aware of the problem which you are solving, or will you need to educate them about it? Where do they go to learn about it, if anywhere?

> **Class discussion**
> The difference between known and unknown problems.

> **120 seconds:**
> If they know about the problem, how are they dealing with it right now? If they don't, how is it affecting them?

Instead of expecting everyone to know how to reach the final goal, you help guide them with small sub-tasks. Beyond helping support the new and inexperienced, the step-by-step structure also simplifies timekeeping and facilitation by ensuring that the whole class is doing the same thing at the same time. Plus, it gives you an easy opportunity to inject little bits of instruction, commentary, guidance, and discussion between each of the sub-steps.

Depending on your available time and the importance of the skill in question, you may want to run several "try it now" exercises which all reinforce the same skill. With each repetition, as your students become more proficient, you can reduce the level of assistance[13] (and/or increase the complexity of the task) to keep them in that sweet spot of learning where they can succeed—but only just. That's where learning happens.

---

[13] Again, if you're interested in reading more about the theory, this concept of temporary educational support—reduced over time to keep students in the ZPD—is called Scaffolding.

You'll never have enough workshop time to advance a group all the way from novice through to mastery. But that's okay, and you don't actually need to carry them that far. You just need to get them to the point where they feel comfortable enough to start trying it for themselves—and making mistakes for themselves—in the real world.

Format 5: Scenario challenges for critical thinking, evaluation, judgement, and decision-making

In a "try it now", you tell everyone what they need to do. In a scenario challenge, you ask them to figure out what they *ought* to do. The former builds skill; the latter, judgement.

You can't *force* a student to spontaneously become a critical thinker. But that doesn't render you powerless to help them get there. Here's how Dr. Kenneth McAlpine, Academic Curriculum Manager at Abertay University, thinks about it:

> *"True, you can't teach experience or good judgment, but you can provide opportunities for students to gain that experience, and, perhaps more importantly, to reflect upon it."*

The very simplest version of a scenario challenge is a prompt to decide, "What would you do if _____?". This small group task would then be followed by class-wide discussion.

For example, let's say you were helping skilled chefs begin their journey toward becoming a *head* chef who is responsible for a whole restaurant. Straightforward Scenario Challenges could include:

- The shipment has been lost for a crucial ingredient and you can't get more in time. How do you respond? Why do you do it that way? How do you prepare the staff and inform the customers (if at all)?
- A server drops a tray of expensive steaks on their way out to the diners. What happens? How do you react to solve the immediate issue and what do you do afterwards (if anything)?

At a slightly deeper level, you can begin by sharing a complex scenario, and then progress through several stages of challenges, like this:

- **Scenario:** Here's a menu marked up with the profit margins of each dish, the preparation time, and their popularity. The restaurant is losing money.
- **Challenge 1: Evaluation:** What's the problem with the current menu? Identify the biggest issues in your groups, and then we'll talk about it as a class.
- **Challenge 2: Decision:** Given the above, what would you do to fix the menu and improve the restaurant's long-term profitability? Again, work in groups and then we'll discuss as a class.

As seen here, the challenge itself is often split into two distinct pieces. The first task is about evaluating the situation, identifying what matters, and demonstrating insight about the situation itself. Pausing for a class-wide discussion at this point will help recover any groups who are stuck in a dead-end while also allowing you to chime in with some relevant insights of your own.

The second task is about decision and action. Given the insights and understanding that have been gathered and discussed in the previous step, what would they do next? How would they move forward? What are the trade-offs? And again, you'll follow this task with a class-wide discussion.

Here's a Scenario Challenge I used in a session with a group of entrepreneurial scientists to help them start thinking about business strategy and product roadmaps based on their research and inventions:

- **Scenario:** You have a breakthrough technology with many wonderful applications. The technology is proven and works, but there are so many possible markets, customers, and applications that you really aren't sure where to start. *(At this point, I give each group a paper handout with full details about the technology and its possible applications).*
- **Challenge 1: Evaluation:** What are the biggest risks and priorities that you would be worried about, if this was your business? Make a list of all the crucial questions.
- **Class-wide discussion:** What has everyone judged as crucial? Why those things and not others? This also allows you to add commentary and suggestions about what they might have overlooked. *(As they mention salient risks, I'm writing a list on the whiteboard or flipchart for them to refer to during the next task.)*
- **Challenge 2: Decision:** Given all of the above, how would you spend your team's time and what would you try to do in the next week, quarter, and year?
- **Class-wide discussion**: Chatting through their choices, the implications thereof, and situations where alternatives might have been stronger. Plus, a general wrap-up to the exercise.

These longer Scenario Challenges are brilliantly engaging (if designed well) and can easily act as the backbone for an entire 45-90 minute section of your workshop. Of course, it will still feel fresh from your student's perspective since it shifts continually between explanation, group work, and class discussion.

Simple scenarios may be able to fit on a slide. More complex ones will generally require a paper handout for teams to review at their own pace.

Although good scenario challenges can take a bit of preparation to design, they're infinitely reusable once you've made them. Facilitating this sort of exercise is both easy and rewarding, since you're mostly just leaving the attendees alone to wrestle with an interesting challenge. And despite being largely hands-off to facilitate, good challenges are extremely high-energy and fun for attendees.

Lessons learned (for the five essential Teaching Formats):

- Lectures should support your Learning Outcomes and help extract lessons-learned from other Teaching Formats, but shouldn't overstay their welcome
- Small group and pair discussion allow students to wrestle with *clear questions* with *ambiguous answers*
- Q&A has a ton of problems, but should still be included after each Learning Outcome (or before each break) to catch misunderstandings and act as a schedule spring
- "Try it now" builds skills through a bit of hands-on practice, though the prompt must be carefully refined to be neither too easy nor too hard
- Scenario Challenges help foster judgement and critical thinking by asking students to understand,

evaluate, and decide how to act in a difficult situation

Design your exercises and refine your schedule

Let's review where we're up to:

- You have a vague topic of what you're meant to be teaching, plus an Audience Profile of who is likely to be in the room.
- You've then clarified that topic into a small set of sharp, focused Learning Outcomes, which have been expanded into a short outline with some supporting arguments or key ideas.
- You've fit these points within the constraints of your schedule by first dividing the available time into rough Schedule Chunks (with good breaks!) and then smooshing the two together (and potentially trying a different arrangement if the first attempt seems too ridiculous).

You then got familiar with the 5 core Teaching Formats:

- **Lectures** (for delivering "book knowledge" and extracting takeaways from exercises)

- **Small group and pair discussions** (for wrestling with ambiguous options and personal implications)
- **"Try it now"** practice (for building hands-on skills)
- **Scenario challenges** (for building wisdom, evaluation, judgement, and decision-making)
- **Question & answer** (for catching major objections/confusion and adding some flexibility into your schedule)

You're now ready to your workshop's exciting high points: its exercises.

Add exercises and build your detailed schedule

Exercise design begins by picking a Teaching Format, filling in some facilitation details, and then designing the full prompt and any supporting materials. However, you won't go through this full process one-at-a-time for each exercise. Instead, you'll work across the whole workshop in a series of passes, going slightly deeper on each pass while maintaining a high-level view of how the whole thing is shaping up and fitting together.

You'll be using your Workshop Outline or Skeleton as a base for exercise design. After all, each item on the Outline is a takeaway of some sort, which means that each item could be either taught by or supported with an exercise in one of the non-lecture Teaching Formats.

Scan for essential exercises: Begin by scanning the outline for any takeaways which *must* be taught by a certain Teaching Format. For example, if one of your

.ng Outcomes (or its supporting points) depends hands-on or practical skill, then you're almost cer-.ly going to need to use some sort of "try it now" ercise in that section.

My shorthand for this task is "knowledge/skill/wisdom" (K/S/W), where knowledge is taught by lecture, skill by "try it now", and wisdom (or judgement or decision-making or evaluation or whatever you want to call it) is taught by scenario challenges. So, going through your Outline or Skeleton, mark each line with either a K, S, or W.

For each S(kill) and W(isdom), try to come up with the broad strokes of either a "try it now" or scenario challenge, respectively. Without one of these hands-on exercises, you'll be "teaching yoga with a lecture" and will have a very hard time getting these lessons to stick. (If you're unable to find a suitable exercise, there are a few extra specialized Formats in the Appendix which might be helpful.)

For each K(nowledge), try to think up a potential topic for a small group discussion. What are the personal implications, applications, or questions around this piece of knowledge? Is there a meaty and interesting discussion to be had around not the knowledge itself, but the implications of that knowledge to the people in the room?

Redraw your schedule. Remember the timeline you drew when combining your Schedule Chunks with your Learning Outcomes? Sketch out another one, and this time mark where your exercises might fall. You can expect to spend 5-15 minutes per exercise, depending on whether you want to include the facilitation extras like a Stand and Share, adding your own commentary, and giving teams time to say hello to each other before the exercise.

Search for (and fix) long lecture segments. On timeline, search for periods of time where you've more than about 20 minutes of lecture in a row. The spots are likely to be a drain on the audience's energy and feel like a drag. You don't need to fix every single one of them, but the more you can fix, the better.

One solution is to reorder your material to end up with either an exercise or a break splitting up the lecture. Another is to insert an "optional" exercise which isn't strictly necessary, but which fits well-enough and can plausibly support the surrounding Learning Outcomes. Small group discussion is the most common candidate here, but you can use any of the Formats for this purpose.

Add Q&A and other supporting activities. Now's as good a time as any to start placing your Q&A sections. Remember that they also function as flexible schedule springs to help recover time if you're running late. As such, I like to aim for about 15 minutes per 90-minute chunk. This can either be one long block right before the coffee break, or 5ish minutes after each Learning Outcome within that chunk.

If you'd like to use either a Post Up or Dot Vote, now's also a good time to get those exercises onto the schedule.

As before, give the overall schedule a sanity check and search for potential Format Fatigue from using the same Format (especially lecture) for too long without any variation. Continue this process of adjusting the schedule and exercises until you're happy with the overall shape.

This is your detailed schedule and is the final ingredient of a 100% finished Workshop Skeleton. At this point, you should be able to get a fairly accurate sense of what your workshop is going to "feel" like on the day-of. In particular, ensure it has these two shining virtues:

1. The Teaching Formats "match" the Learning Outcomes, which avoids the trap of over-relying on lecture and maximizes the chance that the lesson will stick
2. There's lots of variation between different Formats, which will go a long way toward maintaining strong energy levels

If you've got those two qualities on your schedule, then your workshop design is finished and you're ready to start creating the supporting materials: first your exercise details, and then your slides.

Decide on the facilitation details for your exercises

Designing exercises is mostly about picking your Teaching Formats. Once you've got that, you rattle through a checklist of additional facilitation details, which typically includes the following elements:

- Prompt or task ("Discuss this case study, think about X, and decide on Y")
- Group size ("Working in pairs")
- Task time limit ("Five minutes")
- Facilitation extras ("Followed by a stand & share and class discussion")
- Supporting materials, if any (Case study delivered as a paper handout)

- Total exercise time (15 minutes total to introduce, run, stand & share, and discuss)

The only thing left (which we'll get to shortly) is making the slides to tell the students what they're supposed to be doing.

> **Workshop Design Task**: On your workshop outline, mark up each line (i.e. either a Learning Outcome or a Key Idea) with a "K", "S", or "W" to identify whether it is knowledge, skill, wisdom, or some combination thereof.

> **Workshop Design Task:** For each line of your outline, start coming up with possible Teaching Formats (and potentially even specific exercises) which match its category of knowledge/skill/wisdom.

Lessons learned:

- To design workshop exercises, start with a Teaching Format and then add a prompt, timing, grouping, and facilitation details
- With the addition of exercises to your workshop outline, you've pretty much got a completed Workshop Skeleton

Begin with the bare minimum number of slides

Slides take a ton of time to create and often fail in their purpose. They don't fail because they're ugly or overcrowded, but because they obstruct (or at least don't support) your Learning Outcomes.

Used properly, slides serve a clear set of goals:

- For the **facilitator**, slides help keep you on-track, ensure you don't skip major points, let you know when you're falling behind schedule, and remind you to pause for exercises and discussions
- For the **attendees**, slides clarify the major takeaways, remind them of exercise instructions, reduce some of the stress around taking notes, and improve comprehension for non-native speakers

Folks tend to make too many slides. They spend too long on them, and then the pile of slides hurts instead of helping by causing them to run late when they try to "get through everything".

My preferred solution is to begin by creating only the absolute minimum number of essential (or at least very high value) slides, and then cautiously expanding from there.

These essential slides include:

1. Summaries of your Learning Outcomes and supporting arguments
2. Exercise prompts (instructions, rules, discussion topics, etc.)
3. Resource lists (recommended books, your contact info, etc.)

And if you're teaching a topic which demands it:

4. Visual examples for fundamentally visual topics (fashion, architecture, etc.)

That's it. Anything else is a nice-to-have, added later for flavor or style. The classic mistake with slides is to put every single thing you intend to say onto a slide, which then lures you into a mode of narrating the slides to the audience. Your slides should guide and support you, not dictate every sentence that comes out of your mouth.

Note that although the examples in this section are *aesthetically* minimal, that's not strictly required, and you're free to make beautiful slides if you prefer. But if you *are* planning on making them beautiful, delay doing so until after you've laid down the essential content for the whole deck. The more work you've put into the aesthetics of your slides up front, the harder they are to adjust and delete as you refine your workshop.

So, how many slides is "minimum"? The answer will depend on the number of Learning Outcomes and exercises in your workshop. As an example, I recently built a 2-hour workshop with 4 major Learning Outcomes. I ended up with 33 must-have slides:

- 15 summary slides for the crucial takeaways
    - 4 for my main Learning Outcomes
    - 11 for additional key ideas and supporting arguments
- 15 slides for exercise prompts
    - 9 for small group tasks
    - 2 for individual work
    - 4 for full-room discussions
- 3 slides listing resources
    - 1 with suggested reading
    - 2 with my contact details (standard intro/outro slides)

These slides are "essential" in the sense that the workshop would be worse—and harder to facilitate—without them. They are the bare minimum needed to effectively communicate your Learning Outcomes and to help keep both yourself and your audience on track with exercises.

Building the essential slides should take less than an hour. If that sounds impossible, it's because you either a) haven't put together a real Skeleton, so you're designing your workshop from inside the slide software, or b) you're fiddling with style and layout. Both are huge time traps. Come back to the style later in a single pass. If you're not sure what a slide needs to say at any given point, close your laptop and go back to figuring it out on your paper skeleton. It's far too easy to spend dozens of hours fiddling with your slides' details when you should be figuring out the fundamentals.

We'll now take a quick look at each of the three types of essential slides: Learning Outcome summaries, exercise prompts, and resource lists.

Essential slide 1: Learning Outcome summaries

Learning Outcome summary slides come directly from your previously-created Skeleton. This is not the time to go back into improvisational mode. You've already (hopefully) spent the time to decide what's important for folks to learn. Trust your earlier decision and simply move those points into your slide deck. It's the fastest way to get to a good-enough first version of your complete deck and prevents you from getting bogged down.

While Learning Outcome summary slides can come in any number of forms, don't be afraid to keep it simple. After all, not every slide needs to have a bullet point list on it. Depending on the particulars of the takeaway, a summary slide could look like this:

> **Customers matter!**
>
> **A business without customers is just a hobby.**

> **Use The Mom Test to ask good questions**
>
> 1. Ask about **their life**, not your idea
> 2. Specifics in the past, not hypotheticals in the future
> 3. Talk less, listen more
>
> If possible, don't even mention your product and its features.
>
> THE MOM TEST

You'll show one of these slides while concluding each talking point or takeaway from your Skeleton. It's a chance for you to pause, summarize, and check for confusion. I also like to use these slides as the backdrop for focused bits of Q&A. ("Here's what we just covered; any questions or concerns with any of this stuff?")

Learning Outcome slides are helpful for you as a facilitator because they force you to explicitly state your message. And it's helpful for your attendees to see what they're supposed to be learning, laid bare and without all the fun and fluff of your speaking style. If they take notes of what they see on your slides (which is common), then they'll end up with a handy little list of all your Learning Outcomes. And this, conveniently, is exactly what you want them to take away.

Essential slide 2: Exercise prompts

You'll need at least one prompt slide for every exercise. (People *never* understand the task if you only tell them verbally.) If the exercise involves group formation, finish forming groups before you show them the slide which explains what they're supposed to be doing.

Prompts must be short enough to legibly fit on one slide while also being comprehensive enough to resolve any disagreement or confusion within the group. This requires some delicate copywriting and is something to iterate and refine over time as you identify the ways in which participants seem to get lost.

Just like Learning Outcome summary slides, prompt slides don't need to be terribly text-heavy or complicated:

What types of customers are you close to?

Write down:
2 hobbies you enjoy
2 communities you're a part of
2 industries you have experience in

If the prompt is too complex to fit on a slide, then it's possible that you've combined multiple tasks (i.e. drawing the owl) and can split them apart into separate steps, each with its own slide and timer. Or, if the complexity is unavoidable, then consider moving the details onto a paper handout.

Prompts should remain on screen for the entirety of the task. You'd be absolutely shocked at how often attendees seem to "forget" what they're doing and need to re-read the prompt to continue working. This means that you shouldn't use the projector screen for anything else during an exercise (like showing a timer or image).

That's it. Still, it's worth giving your prompt slides a few extra editing passes since bad ones will invariably introduce workshop-delaying confusion.

Essential slide 3: Resources lists (and intro/outro)

Attendees adore lists of resources: recommended books, blogs, tools, where to learn more, etc. As soon as you put one of these resource lists up on screen, everyone will start frantically taking notes and snapping pictures. While lengthy lists may require a paper handout, shorter ones can fit on a slide. A resource list is rarely required for your workshop to succeed, but it's a nice way to wrap things up and acts as a high-value takeaway.

You'll also need an intro and outro slide with the talk's title, your contact information, and an optional call-to-action to ask attendees to do something like send you an email, perform a homework task, go to a website, or buy something.

Although your deck is still very bare-bones at this point, it has everything needed to keep your exercises and Learning Outcomes on track. And as such, you can rest easy in the knowledge that if you run out of prep time, what you've already built will be more than sufficient for you to succeed.

> **Workshop Design Task (30-60 minutes):** Create your essential slides without worrying about style or layout. This includes Learning Outcome (and supporting argument) summary slides, exercise and discussion prompts, an intro/outro, and optional resource lists.

Sprinkle on the flavor slides

All that being said, a bit of flavor can really help the overall feel of your workshop. Once you're happy with your Skeleton and have built the essentials, you can spend as much (or as little) time as you like making them beautiful, personal, and fun, as well as adding extra nice-to-have slides.

While there are any number of ways to add flavor to your deck, one that's particularly useful is a series of slides that build up toward a Learning Outcome or key idea. Often, during a lecture segment, you'll use a bit of creative storytelling, metaphor, or examples. These narrative stepping-stones are excellent candidates for some extra (non-essential) slides to help carry the story and illustrate the plot.

For example, you might be making the observation—in a session about product design—that something which is *beautiful* is not necessarily also *functional*. And you might choose to illustrate this point by comparing a common and effective juicer against the one which won all the design awards despite being completely awful to use:

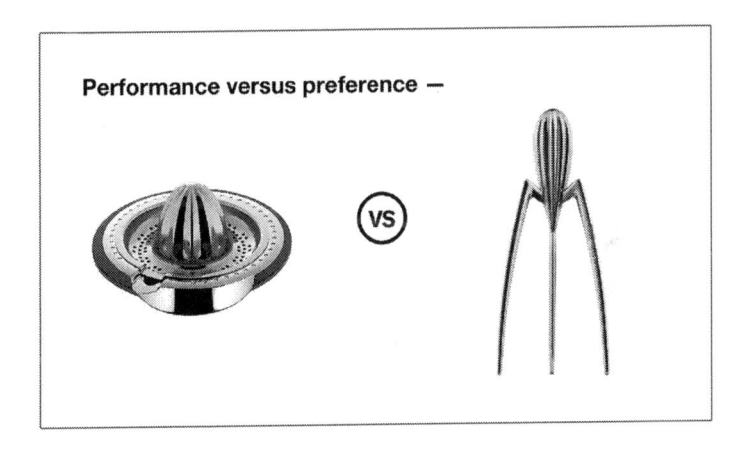

Performance versus preference —

(VS)

These sorts of slides break up the tempo of your lecture and can get a laugh. But be careful to use them for a purpose. Some facilitators go flavor-crazy, and the purpose of their talk gets lost in its attempt to be entertaining. It's like cooking: the spices should support the dish, not overwhelm it. (The flavor is becoming a problem if it's messing with your timings by causing you to spend too long on takeaways which don't warrant so much time relative to the rest of your material.)

No matter how you choose to teach a particular Learning Outcome—whether via lecture, challenge, exercise, discussion, or whatever else—remember that the Learning Outcome comes first. Slides are built to serve.

You are never obligated to include an image

Images are a double-edged sword. When used properly to directly support a talking point, they can enhance the message or deliver a punchline. But facilitators often feel obligated to include an image on every slide, which leads to a doomed quest for mediocre stock photography and ends up distracting from your talk instead of adding to it.

Superfluous images backfire. Every time an image appears on your slides, people look at it, shifting their attention away from you and what you're saying. If the image is delivering your core message, then this is fine. But whenever you include an inessential image just to "look nice", you're guaranteeing that your whole audience will spend several seconds trying to interpret what it means, when you'd prefer that they just be listening to you. Even something as "neutral" as an image of a landscape will still dominate your audience's attention while they try to figure out why it's there.

Also, never use sexy images to try to be controversial or engaging. I know this sounds ridiculous, but you'd be surprised how often presenters try something saucy to "keep the audience paying attention". It backfires frequently and badly. Much better to just design a good workshop which keeps the energy high without resorting to cheap tricks.

Images are great, but only if they support your talking points. Never include them simply because you're scared of leaving empty space on a slide. A slide's design should serve its content, and your content should never be fluffed out to fill an arbitrary slide template.

> White space on slides is not a problem

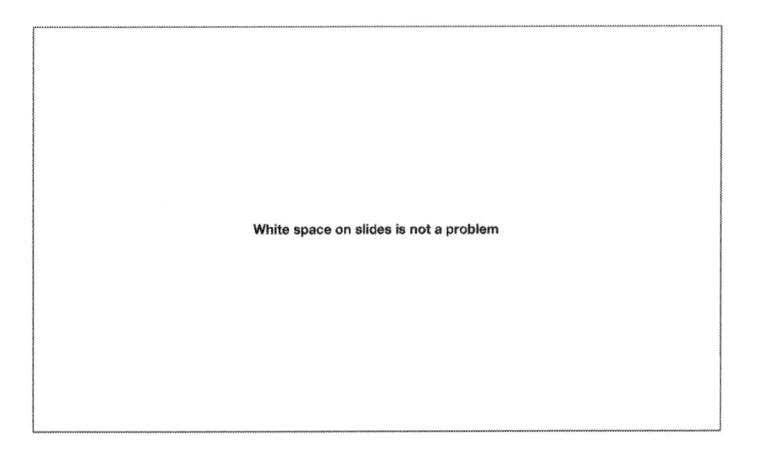

Titles should contain the message, not the topic

Too often, slide titles say nothing of value. Instead, they act as a vague "topic" introducing and describing the slide without actually conveying any information. But that's silly. A slide's title is its most valuable real estate and should therefore contain the most important part of the message. Here's the text from a slide which has fallen for this trap:

```
Sales 101

   - Sales is about asking good ques-
     tions
   - What you're learning is more im-
     portant than what you're pitching
```

```
-   If you're doing all the talking,
    then you're failing
```

Look at the title: "Sales 101." It's wasting the most valuable, most visible, highest-priority spot on the slide with a line of text which is absolutely devoid of any useful information. If you ask me the secret of sales, and I lean in, confidentially, and whisper, "Sales 101," then you'd be right to roll your eyes and walk away.

To make better use of the natural hierarchy of a slide's title and contents, the first bullet can be promoted to take the old title's place, since that first point is really the main message of this slide:

```
Sales is about asking good questions:

-   What you're learning is more im-
    portant than what you're pitching
-   If you're doing all the talking,
    then you're failing
```

This critique may seem weirdly specific, but it's a *super* common mistake. And it's also more impactful than it seems, since it leads to a stilted speaking style where you find yourself "introducing" every new slide instead of just getting to the point. With a slide like the first one, a speaker is tempted to say,

> "Okay, now I'm going to talk about Sales 101 (a nebulous sentence with no value). The most important thing you need to know (an empty transition which was forced thanks to the previous sentence) is that sales is about asking good questions... (finally we're on to the real material)"

Whereas with the second version, it feels natural to cut the fluff and simply begin with:

"Sales is about asking good questions… (straight to the value)"

Plus, if an attendee is trying to follow along with your slides, the first version delays and (slightly) confuses them, whereas the second version is crystal clear about what they're supposed to be learning.

I think the reason this mistake is so widespread is that folks design their slides before defining their Learning Outcomes, so they end up titling their slides with vague topics instead of their real message. To avoid this trap, design a good Skeleton first and then put the main message into your slide titles. If that makes the rest of the slide feel too empty, fear not! Simply switch the slide template to something which highlights the important stuff even more:

> **Sales is about asking good questions.**

> **Workshop design task** (10-20 minutes): Flip through your slide deck and search for slide titles which don't say anything. What's the point you're really trying to make with that slide? If possible, promote that to be the title. If that makes the rest of the slide feel "empty", then perhaps you can try deleting everything else and putting the title front and center. While you're at it, also consider deleting any "filler" images and stock photography which distract without informing.

Lessons learned:

- Your first pass on a slide deck should contain only the absolute essentials (Learning Outcome summaries, exercise prompts, intro/outro and resource lists, and visual examples)
- Once you have the essentials in place, you can (optionally) add fun, nice-to-have slides which offer examples, storytelling, and personality

Summary of Part 1

Start by defining your Audience Profile (who):

- Describes who is attending the workshop
- How experience they are
- Why they are bothering to show up
- Any concerns or objections the audience may have

Next, insert breaks to divide the available time into Schedule Chunks (when):

- Draft your schedule quickly by first allocating your coffee and lunch breaks
- 60-90 minutes of workshop between breaks is the sweet spot

Given those constraints, decide on the concrete Learning Outcomes and takeaways (what):

- Learning Outcomes are the sharp, specific, high-value takeaways that the audience has shown up for
- Add supporting arguments to each Learning Outcome to highlight key ideas or talking points

Combine into a Workshop Skeleton:

- Complete your Workshop Skeleton by inserting your Learning Outcomes into your Schedule Chunks
- Remix and cut content until everything fits into the Chunks

Pick the best Teaching Formats to maintain education, energy, and attention:

- Vary teaching formats at least every 20 minutes to keep the audience feeling fresh
- Select Teaching Formats that match what is being taught — you can't teach yoga with a lecture
- Lectures are great for delivering "book" knowledge and addressing takeaways from exercises
- Small group & pair discussions allow audiences to engage with topics from lectures
- "Try it now" exercises allow new skills to be practiced
- Scenario challenges develop critical thinking and decision-making.
- Question & answer sections add flexibility to your schedule

Before getting stuck in style and layout, create the most essential slides:

- A slide deck only needs to contain the absolute essentials — less is more in a workshop
- Essential slides include summarizing Learning Outcomes and supporting arguments; exercise prompts; and important resource lists
- Flavor slides are fun, nice-to-have visual that enhance examples, storytelling, and personality

Closing thoughts on workshop design

Hey there, it's Devin. One of my first professional teaching gigs was training non-programmers to program. (Creatively titled "Programming for Non-Programmers".)

On paper, it should have been a cakewalk: I was comfortable in front of an audience, the materials had already been prepared (mostly lectures with some large practice exercises), and the tickets had already been sold. All I had to do was to stand up front and lead the audience through the magical journey of launching their first website. But 30 minutes into the first session, it was clear that I had already lost the whole class, who seemed to just be silently mouthing "huh?" over and over again.

Being unable, at the time, to recognize the deep flaws in the workshop's underlying design, I pushed forward the only way I knew: an increasingly enthusiastic—but ultimately doomed—delivery. Although a few of them did walk away having learned a thing or two, the majority left drained and bored. It was a big failure and a major wake-up call. A great workshop is so much more than just being an enthusiastic lecturer. The design is paramount.

Suffice to say, the workshop was broken. But it was broken in ways which you would now be able to recognize and fix: long lectures about practical skills (I can't believe I seriously tried to teach programming without programming), followed by too-vague, too-long exercises which required constant 1-on-1 assistance for every single student.

Over subsequent iterations, I tore up and reworked the whole Skeleton: sharper Learning Outcomes, better choice of Teaching Formats, clearer exercises, and a far more pleasant energy level throughout the day. Much like how a fledgling chef is told to "let the knife do the work", I had started to design a workshop that did the teaching for me instead of relying on my personal performance alone.

A few sessions later, this workshop had become hugely effective for the students, and second nature for me. Far from the stressful, overwhelming experience of fighting against the originally flawed design, these full days of teaching were even starting to become *pleasant*.

And now that you're up to speed with the essentials of good workshop design, I think you too will find the facilitation to be far easier than you expect—and perhaps even a little bit fun. Coming up next, we'll turn out attention to the question of how to do it.

Part two:
Facilitation Essentials

In Part 2, we'll cover facilitation chronologically, beginning with how to introduce yourself and continuing with how to start an exercise, keep it moving, and recover everyone's attention once it's finished. We'll then get into how to deal with common challenges like slipped schedules, hostile audiences, and your own fatigue.

In general, facilitation is easier than you think. After all, folks have shown up because they want to learn something, which means that they want both you and your workshop to succeed. They're rooting for you. And with a little bit of facilitation know-how, you'll be able to keep it all on track.

How to introduce yourself without making everyone hate you

I recently attended a beer tasting — hard to screw up, right? But the host mysteriously chose *not* to begin by handing us a tasty beer. Instead, she fell into the common trap of trying too hard to justify her reason for being there by using a long, overwrought intro. She talked about her passion for beer and her trips through the hops fields and her childhood experience of tasting the foam from her father's brew... She'd clearly been watching too many inspirational internet talks and had lost sight of what her event was really about: attendees tasting beers.

The purpose of your intro is to offer *just enough* credibility for the audience to give you the benefit of the doubt and let you start delivering the value they showed up for. In the case of a workshop, the "value" is in delivering your first high-impact Learning Outcome. In the case of a beer tasting, the "value" would have been in the first sip of a surprising and delicious beer.

Remember, the audience has generally chosen to be there, and thus already believes that you're credible. As such, you don't need to beat them over the head with your CV, work history, or life story.

Of course, you do still need to tell them who you are. But it can be quite short, including only a) your name and b) one or two relevant details. Here are a few examples of great personal intros (assuming, of course, that the details being shared are relevant to the topic being taught):

> "Hey, I'm Katie. A few years back I quit my job and spent the next two years as an apprentice woodworker learning traditional furniture making, and now most of my home is filled with stuff I've made myself."

> "Hey, I'm Sophie. I've trained and managed high-value sales teams in a number of Fortune 500s, and at the peak was responsible for delivering $400 million per year in partnership-driven sales."

> "Hey, I'm Jacob. I've never done this stuff professionally, but I've worked on a bunch of hobby projects over the years, and I wanted to share some of my lessons-learned from trying to apply all the advice and best practices from the 'experts'."

> "Hey, I'm Ian. I've spent two decades freelancing, although now I'm primarily a full-time dad for my two boys. I'm going to talk about how to fit freelancing into your life without sacrificing on either side."

> "Hey, I'm Imran. I'm a data analyst and have recently been helping optimize a bunch of Facebook ad campaigns. I've seen that with a bit of patience and the right approach, you can usually increase your campaigns' initial performance by 10-20x."

All of these are great: one key piece of relevant information, chosen and presented in a way which suggests you have something worth saying. If you have a brilliant stamp of credibility (like Sophie's huge sales number or a Nobel Prize), then by all means, mention it. But the other examples work fine without anything like that, because they've packaged up whatever experience they *do* have into a clear, focused explanation of why they're worth listening to.

So, what about our misguided beer host? If I were in her shoes, I might try something like this for the next event:

> *"Hey, I'm Jackie. I used to be a wine sommelier, but I've always loved—and have recently been obsessing over—beer. Today I'm excited to share a few of the most interesting I've found, all produced locally around Barcelona."*

When it comes to intros, short is good. You can add in more personal details later, during the workshop itself, if and when those details are applicable to the Learning Outcome at hand.

At a slightly more advanced level, you can placate skeptical and unwilling audiences by tailoring your (still short) intro toward their biggest objection. For example, imagine I'm teaching a sales workshop to a group of technical folks who are deeply suspicious of salespeople. To help alleviate their concerns, I might say:

> *"Hey, I'm Rob. I'm a programmer who was forced to learn sales in my first business. It was a tough couple years since there aren't many sales books written for introverted techies. But it turns out it's actually pretty*

straightforward once you know how to do it, and you don't need to turn into some sort of pushy sales guy."

That's enough. It shows that I understand their concerns and their world, and that I might be worth listening to even though they aren't too keen on the broader topic. They're now a bit more likely to give me the benefit of the doubt and wait to hear what I have to say. And then I can jump straight into delivering value.

Now imagine that I'm teaching the same material, but to a sales-friendly crowd who is more worried about my personal experience and credibility. In that case, I might instead introduce myself this way:

"Hey I'm Rob. I've been running startups for about 10 years, have been through YC,[14] and have raised funding in both the US and UK. I've bankrupted a couple businesses—which isn't much fun—and have had better results with the more recent ones. We're going to be talking about what we can do to avoid the bad results and get the good ones by changing the way we think about sales."

Crafting these sorts of tailored intros relies on having a clear Audience Profile (which we covered at the start of Part 1). If possible, I'll even ask the event organizer to predict the crowd's most likely concern, or I'll try to get a sense of it during a few minutes of pre-event chit chat.

In terms of your intro's tone, never joke that you're tired, hungover, or unprepared. The audience is giving up their time to be there. Humility and self-deprecation

---

[14] YCombinator is a prestigious startup program which I'll name-drop for certain audiences who require a stamp of credibility. It's the startup version of "casually" mentioning you went to Harvard.

are fine, but don't imply that you're disrespecting their time. On that note, it's a mistake to go too far with the self-deprecation. Self-deprecation only works when counterbalanced against the audience already believing that you're great. I'm not saying you need to pretend to be amazing at everything, but do give them a teacher they can believe in.

Lessons learned:

- The purpose of an intro isn't to summarize your life or CV, but to give the audience *just enough* for them to start listening to you
- When facing a skeptical audience, tailor your (still short) intro toward their biggest concern
- Get through it quickly and start delivering the value folks showed up for

Don't treat your audience as bigger than it is

Your facilitation needs to be right-sized. If you're running a session for 10 people seated around a single table, you might want to take a seat yourself and to use a more conversational tone than you would when standing on stage with a microphone. On the other hand, if you have 1,000 attendees in a large event, it would be a fool's errand to tell folks to interrupt you whenever they have questions.[15]

Think of yourself as a party host:

Fewer than 12 attendees is a dinner party. By the end of the session, you're going to be able to understand every single person and address their individual concerns. The energy level may not be frenetic, but that doesn't mean people aren't fully engaged, attentive, and happy to be there. You are the host of this dinner party, and while you certainly *can* give firm

---

[15] With very large audiences, the only folks who will actually interrupt you are self-promoting sociopaths intent on stealing your audience to do some off-topic showboating.

instructions ("Get to your seats please, it's time for dessert!"), you can also just sit alongside and talk to them in a normal, conversational tone.

12–20 attendees is a birthday dinner. It's a little bit rowdier, so sometimes you'll need to stand up and demand attention to make yourself heard. That being said, you're still going to have an individual interaction with every person in the room, even if you don't learn every detail of their lives. This sort of size works well in a few clusters of cabaret seating, or with the whole class arranged in a circle of chairs or around a big boardroom table where everyone can talk to each other. And conversely, it's a small enough group that it'd be a little weird if you put them in lecture seating and make them just sit quietly and listen to you all day.

20–50 attendees is a house party. While it's quite likely that you won't get to talk directly to everyone who shows up, that's okay. It's still small enough that attendees feel they can come find you if they have some sort of problem. And apart from that, they're enjoying being at the event you've put together. Depending on how energetic they are, you can sometimes talk to them normally (e.g. going to each cluster of people and asking them to stop pouring so much red wine on the carpet), and other times you might choose to use your authority as a host to seize their attention and address them as a group ("No more red wine, you maniacs!"). This is about the size where your skills in design and facilitation really start to be essential, and you won't be able to run a smooth session without them.

50+ attendees is a wedding. Everyone is there for the same reason, but it's a big enough crowd that you need to be more structured. To be heard, you may need to use a stage and a microphone. This makes it harder for the audience to ask questions, express their concerns, or generally influence the day. Since you aren't able to help everyone individually, the design and execution of the event are absolutely crucial in ensuring everyone has a good time.

The size of your audience determines your tone as well as the technique you'll use to get their attention. At a 20-person dinner party, you can just say "Hey everyone" and you're pretty much done. If someone is still having a private conversation, it's easy to single them out and bring them back into the group. But not so much at a 50-person wedding reception. This is why getting everyone's attention by banging a spoon against your glass seems acceptable at a wedding, but a little strange at a smaller gathering. You need to use a tone and technique appropriate to the size of the group.

Going individual

In addition to being right-sized, remember that even large crowds are still composed of individuals. There's a massive temptation—especially for newer facilitators—to treat every audience as a gigantic, anonymous, homogeneous crowd. It feels safer, somehow.

I remember spectating a workshop with a total of five attendees, all sitting around a single table no larger than you'd find in a dining room. The facilitator—to his credit—had designed an amazing workshop, and two of the attendees were so engaged in the exercises that they kept failing to hear him announce that it was time to move on. But instead of saying, "Hey James, Jackie, bring it back in," he would raise his voice and start yelling at the sky: "THAT IS TIME, EVERYONE STOP. TIME IS UP. STOP WORKING." Meanwhile, the other three students (who *were* paying attention) were justifiably beginning to suspect that their teacher was a crazy person.

What he didn't appreciate is that up until about 30 attendees, crowd control is generally fastest and most effective if you treat distracted participants as *individuals*.

For an explanation of why, consider the following common scenario: your attendees are working in groups and you find yourself needing to give them a bit of further instruction. The typical approach is to treat them as a crowd: gathering everyone's collective attention, telling everyone what you have to say, and then setting them all back to work. That's fine, but fairly labor-intensive. Instead, so long as you have fewer than about 10 groups, you could just walk through the room, stopping at each cluster and telling them what to do next. The groups will end up slightly out of phase with each other (by as long as it takes you to walk through the room) but will all be guaranteed to receive the new instruction with zero delay or friction.

Another common scenario is to have given a set of instructions to the class but failed to reach a small number of distracted individuals. Many teachers will delay the entire class until they've recovered these few, when a far better option is often to let the bulk of the class get started and then walk over to the off-track individuals to scoot them forward by hand.[16]

If you really need *everyone's* silence and attention, then you can single out the relevant individuals by name or walk over and tap them on the shoulder while telling them (in a normal speaking voice) that it's time to move on to whatever's next. You never want to scold your attendees as if they are children (which *decimates* goodwill), but it's fine to respectfully address them as an individual.

Make a habit of going individual during every exercise. Once you've assigned the task, don't just stay in your teaching area. Instead, walk through the room, visiting each group to watch and listen to them work, checking on their progress and scanning for problems. If you see that they're stuck on something, it's a chance to proactively unstick them without having to rely on a student being willing to ask a question in front of the whole class.

We'll look at more advanced approaches to crowd control a bit later, which can be used to manage larger audiences. But for now, just remember that every crowd is composed of individuals, and your quickest

---

[16] Think of attendees as energetic puppies, incapable of disrespecting anyone and only getting off-track due to excitement and glee. You don't need to take their distraction personally or try to "establish your authority". Instead, just scoot them back on track in the least disruptive way possible (which sometimes means allowing them to remain distracted while you sort out everyone else).

way to influence the former is often to speak to the latter.

Lessons learned:

- Your style of facilitation should be "right-sized" to match the audience
- It feels safe to always address the entire crowd as a single unit, but it's often faster and more effective to address them as individuals

Seating and group formation

The difference between a brilliant exercise and one which flops will often come down to little more than the friction of your facilitation. And although obsessing over something like chair arrangement and group formation sounds fairly mundane, polishing these seemingly trivial edges will allow you to build a day which flows smoothly, tightly, and effortlessly from one exercise to the next. And this, in turn, helps keep energy levels at their highest.

As simple as it sounds, "Get into groups of 3" is a slow and difficult task for audiences to complete. Although most of the class will be fine, a small subset will take long enough to create a problematic delay for everyone else (and it also risks isolating the shyest and most socially vulnerable participants).

The solution is part room setup and part facilitation:

1. If possible, use a seating arrangement which creates "natural" groups
2. In either case, help organize the grouping yourself and find a home for any isolated individuals

Good seating allows for quick, unambiguous group formation. As such, the chair (and potentially table) layout is *the* most important quality of any teaching venue. For example, if everyone is already sitting at tables of six when you ask them to get into groups of three, then there's really no way for them to end up stranded.

As such, **the absolute best seating is cabaret (clusters of attendees around individual tables) with six people per table.** The magic number of six allows you to rearrange them as pairs, triplets, or a full half-dozen without requiring anyone to switch seats. (But anywhere from 4-8 attendees per table still feels great.) Plus, cabaret makes it easy for you to walk between the tables and listen in on them working during exercises.

Cabaret seating doesn't need to look like formal wedding. Here, students are seated around tables in groups of three or four, ready to get back into groupwork without any delays from group formation.

Of course, you'll often find yourself stuck in nonideal venues. In those cases, you should rearrange it into the least bad version of itself. For example, if the room is set up as a lecture, but with movable chairs, then you can improve group formation by arranging the chairs into loose clusters before the event starts or during a break.

The absolute worst arrangements are lecture auditoriums with fixed seating (especially if they have "movie theatre rows" which prevent people from relocating and turning). In these cases, the best you can do is to scoot everyone toward the front and pack them together, so nobody is stranded without a neighbor. Attendees *hate* being moved after they've already taken a seat, so it's best if you begin doing it while people are first arriving, as opposed to trying to move them after they've already sat down. (You can also simplify the issue by using a bit of tape and paper to barricade the prohibited rows.)

If you *do* need to move them, you'll have to insist on it fairly firmly and be willing to stand your ground until everyone is sitting where you need them. One way to facilitate this is to conceal what you're asking them to do while giving one (polite) instruction at a time. And to continue repeating yourself at each step until everyone has done it. It sounds a bit like a crazy person's rant, but it works:

> *"Everyone stand up. Everyone. Okay. Now pick up your stuff and move out into the aisle. Yep, for real, grab your stuff and get into the aisle. Great. Walk to the front. Come on, get up here—I can't smell that bad. Okay, take a seat in one of the first four rows. Nice, thanks for that and sorry for the shuffle—we're going to be doing some group work so I need you all sitting together."* (All of

this is said with a bit of a playful wink, as opposed to with a demanding or authoritative tone.)

If you just ask them to move and then stop talking, I can 100% guarantee that almost everybody will ignore your request. Instead, you need to dig in your heels and keep talking (and making a bit of a scene of yourself) until everyone is where you need them to be. This sort of rearrangement does take a couple minutes and it does affect your energy levels. But in bad lecture halls, it's generally necessary if you hope to run any exercises at all. (And as mentioned, it's much easier to catch folks when they're first arriving as opposed to trying to fix it later.)

Regardless of the room setup, you should remain on full alert and ready to assist throughout group formation, especially with regards to spotting isolated folks who are having trouble finding a good group. You'll be pleasantly surprised by how quickly you can manually assign groups, even with an audience of 50 or 100 people. All you need to do is gesture toward them and say:

> *"You three, you're together. You lot have too many, so split into two groups of three. You there, leave that group and join those two over there."*

Then scan for stranded individuals and ensure they have a good home. Note that this only works if you've finished forming groups *before* telling them what they're going to be working on. If they already know their task, then you won't have their attention and these sorts of corrections become impossible.

> **Workshop Commandment:** Finish group formation before revealing the task they're going to be working on.

In rooms where it's difficult for folks to move around (like in lecture auditoriums), you won't always be able to fix uneven groups and will need to account for that in your exercise design. As such, if I know I might be dealing with fixed seating, I'll design my exercises to handle flexible group sizes of 2-3 (or 3-5), which usually allows sufficient wiggle room to find a group for everyone without requiring them to shift seats.

In longer workshops (> 2 hours), consider rearranging the groups each time you take a break. Fresh groups help lift the energy, vary the perspectives that folks are exposed to, and also to spread the damage wrought by hostile attendees and group dominators (more on them in a moment).

But changing groups generally requires switching seats, and there's an inertia and social pressure which keeps folks staying put. Plus, people tend to "nest" in their original seats, spreading out their papers and notes and bag all over the place. As such, I like to *force* them to switch seats/tables after each coffee break. Before calling the break, I warn them that they'll be sitting somewhere else when they return, so they might want to consolidate their belongings. And upon returning, I treat the rearrangement as the first "exercise" and facilitate it as if it was any other workshop task.

If you can't (or don't want to) switch their seats, you can still get some of the benefits by just changing the *number* of people per group across exercises. For example, in a series of exercises you might start with triplets, then go down to pairs, then up to groups of six, and so on.

Keep an eye out for group dominators and try to curtail them. The most obvious version is the loud alpha who talks over everyone. When you notice one, just sit down with that group, gently-but-firmly cutting off the alpha and creating space for the contributions of the rest of the group.

A more subtle type of dominator is the "secretary" who acts as an implicit judge and gatekeeper by controlling what gets written down during exercises. This is detectable when only one person is holding a pen or all the exercise notes are written in the same handwriting. In this case, try to get everyone else to pick up a pen and encourage them to "get it written down before you start talking about it."

You usually won't need to be too heavy-handed with any of these folks. Most group dominators are doing it accidentally and will quickly self-correct once you intervene and demonstrate a better group culture. (And for the truly hostile ones... We'll return to them shortly.)

Other venue considerations

Beyond helping with group formation, the venue also influences energy levels. Energy drains faster in bad venues, which means that you and your workshop will need to work harder to compensate. This is less of an issue in short (<2 hour) workshops but can have a significant impact in longer sessions. Apart from seating, bad venues can have a few other shortcomings:

- **No natural light.** Energy drains much faster in a venue with bad (or no) windows.
- **Limited access to coffee.** Made in bulk, coffee is as cheap to produce as water. I don't understand how venues still screw this up, but they do.
- **Limited access to good snacks.** Blood sugar matters. Plus, people skip breakfast and event food is often terribly bad for sustaining energy.
- **Venue distractions.** Noisy coffee machine in the back of the room? Sloppy operations which lead to unexpected delays or interruptions? Missing materials? A door which creaks loudly whenever someone leaves for the bathroom? It all hurts.
- **A too-small space.** Limited wall and table space restrict exercises. Packed seating prevents you from walking the room and rearranging attendees. And being stuck in a single small room for an extended period can make the workshop seem extra monotonous.

Although these sorts of issues probably feel outside of your control, you can dramatically increase your chances of having a good venue through diligent pre-event communications with the client, venue, or organizer. Ask them what your room is like, tell them how you'd like it arranged, and clarify the equipment that you'll need.

If they can't do what you need, then either find ways to work around the constraints or ask if it's possible to switch to a different room. In the worst cases, you may need to adjust your workshop's design to account for the room's shortcomings (for example, by eliminating or adjusting exercises which won't work with the space available, ordering in your own coffee to compensate for bad catering, or lengthening your breaks to let folks walk outside to get some natural light or buy a snack). If the venue is an unknown it's always wise to show up early, just in case you need to rearrange anything before folks arrive.

It's possible to survive (and thrive) within a bad venue, but you'll need to work extra hard to refill attendee energy and attention. On the other hand, a perfect venue—with tons of natural light, great snacks, and seamless operations—can keep the energy topped up practically by itself. Top-tier venues compensate for a lot of mistakes in your workshop design and help ensure that your audience stays at their sharpest.

> **Workshop Design Task** (2-20 minutes): If you've got a workshop coming up, do you know what your room setup will be? If not, who can you call or email to find out? Even better, can you visit it or see a couple pictures? If it has problems, try changing either the room, your facilitation, or the design of the workshop itself.

Lessons learned:

- The best seating arrangements—like cabaret—allow for natural grouping and easy rearrangement
- The worst seating arrangements—like fixed lecture halls—make group formation extremely difficult and you'll need to work hard to overcome such a disadvantage
- Energy levels will stay higher for longer in venues with natural light, readily accessible coffee, snacks, a distraction-free environment, and plenty of space

Getting more from your exercises

As tempting as it can seem, group exercises are not a chance for you to kick back and relax. To unlock an exercise's full educational value, you need to perform two additional facilitation tasks:

1. During the exercise, "walk the room" and listen to the groups working
2. Immediately after the exercise, run a brief "stand and share" discussion

Let's take a quick look at each.

Walk the room to spot unknown-unknowns

During the exercise, you're going to "walk the room" and listen in on the groups doing their work. You'll use what you hear in two crucial ways:

1. Listening to them talk will show you how they've [mis]understood your message, which

allows you to explicitly fix their misconceptions, either individually or when you return to teaching
2. The ideas you overhear will become an anchor for asking them to share their thoughts during "stand and share" presentations after the exercise

There's also a third bonus benefit:

3. Shy and confused students often feel comfortable asking questions when you're nearby that they wouldn't ask in front of the class

You don't need to say anything while walking the room, and you shouldn't join the conversation unless a group has misunderstood the prompt or is stuck in a bad conversational dynamic (e.g. someone is dominating the whole discussion). Instead, just eavesdrop while strolling slowly past. But don't start talking; if you engage in a group's conversation, they'll generally pay deference to you, which degrades that group's "discussion" into a tiny lecture with you at its head.

You'll sometimes find that as soon as you approach, groups will go silent and turn to you, as if awaiting instruction. Or that they'll start directing their questions and comments toward you instead of each other. I like to handle this by staying silent, shrugging in a helpless sort of way, and gesturing back toward their peers. If they still don't get the hint, I just turn and walk away.

That being said, sometimes a student will feel safe enough in this context to ask you an off-topic question which they were too shy to ask in front of the whole class, and which is obviously important to them. This typically reveals a deep need and I think it's worth trying to find a way to help them. If it's a quick and simple question, you can answer it right then. But if it will take more than 10-30 seconds, it's better to let the group continue working by either a) telling the student to follow you away from the group, where you can talk privately, b) suggesting that you chat about it at length during the next coffee break, or c) waiting until the whole class reconvenes and then giving your answer to the anonymous question for everyone to hear.

Walking the room is crucial for spotting unknown-unknowns. Students often *believe* they know something, when they are, in fact, 100% wrong. As such, they'll never be able to explicitly ask you about it. But their confusion will be immediately obvious if you listen to them working and talking, which allows you to intervene.

Once you've repeated a workshop several times, you'll become familiar enough with attendees' thought patterns that you can anticipate and prevent the unknown-unknowns from ever taking root. But in the early iterations, it's usually a matter of listening for confusion during group exercises and then adding a quick verbal correction.

"Stand and share" at the end of each exercise

After each pair/group exercise, you'll want to hear from a subset of the teams. This motivates everyone to work harder for future exercises, but more importantly, it provides a chance to spread good ideas and correct misconceptions. But people are shy, so we'll use a bit of facilitation magic to make it easier for them.

In most cases, you want to "randomly" sample from just two or three groups. Four can start to feel tedious unless the exercise happened to include some unusually interesting and varied results.

The first person who shares will set the tone for everyone else. So rather than ask for a volunteer, I'll single someone out who I know is happy to be the center of attention and whose group seemed to have had plenty to talk about:

> *"You folks back there seemed to have a lively discussion. Susan, would you mind summarizing some of the stuff you were talking about for us?"*

The reason for first singling out a confident student is that you're going to use them to set a (positive) example for everyone else:

> *"Wait wait—could you please stand up where you're at, so we can all see you? And turn to the class—you're talking to them, not me. Perfect. So, what did you end up with?"*

Asking them to stand up and face the class is important. The real benefit is for everyone *else* in the class who is supposed to be listening. If the volunteer simply stays in their seat and talks toward the teacher (as they'll almost always do by default), then every other student in the room will zone out, get distracted, and lose energy. As an added benefit, having a student stand up and address the room will quickly bring all other distracted chit-chat to an end, since people rarely want to be rude to their peers.

After starting with someone talkative to break the ice, my next ideal participant would be an individual or group who hasn't yet spoken up, but who seems alert and engaged. And then any eager volunteers. As mentioned, you don't need to hear from everyone, since that turns into a long drag. The other students will have a chance to share their work after future exercises.

If you'd like to subtly guide the focus of the conversation, you can prime your "volunteer" by asking them about something you overheard while walking the room. This is especially helpful in motivating shy participants to talk, since they'll find it easier to speak when given a more constrained task:

> "I heard the group over there saying something interesting about the drawbacks of digital tools. Jeremy, would you mind standing up and talking us through it?"

You can also springboard off an overheard discussion to go into your own little anecdote or lecture segment. For example, you might say:

> "I heard a few of you talking about X. That's a super common concern, and what people normally do is..."

Although this is technically a monologue, the fact that you've framed it as a response to a group's discussion improves its tone and makes it feel more relevant.

If the class was working on something personal (like career goals), then people can be prohibitively nervous about presenting their own ideas. In addition to using the priming technique mentioned above, you can outmaneuver this reluctance by asking them to present *someone else's* ideas instead of their own. For example:

> "Who overheard something in their group that was interesting or different? (A few hands go up. You single someone out.) You don't need to tell us who said it, but can you tell us a bit about the big idea and why it stood out to you?"

Whether or not this matters will be a bit culture-specific. You probably don't need to bother with this sort of encouragement for an American audience (they're happy taking credit for their own ideas), but you'll find yourself using it constantly when teaching in more reserved countries.

You can also shift the focus away from the *results* of the process and toward the *experience* of the process itself. This involves asking folks to talk about how it felt and whether it worked and what was surprising or interesting about approaching the issue in this particular way. For example:

> *"Who found that experience to be a little bit weird or awkward? Raise of hands? Hah, yeah, I did too, when I was getting started. (Gesturing toward someone) Would you mind trying to describe what felt strange or surprising about it?*

After each "stand and share", I like to lead a quick round of applause. Of course, if you clap for one person, you'll want to clap for everyone else who presents as well, since otherwise the absence of applause implies criticism.

"Stand and share" is one of the reasons that seemingly simple formats (like small group discussion) can end up being so powerful. It's not just the exercise itself, but also the class-wide sharing, discussion, and commentary.

Lessons learned:

- During exercises, walk the room and listen to people working, while being careful to avoid joining the conversation as its "leader"
- After each group exercise, ask a few people to stand and share their thinking (speaking to the class, not you)

Answering student questions

While student questions can (and will) pop up at any point throughout the workshop, they're especially common during the chatty discussion which follows a lively exercise. Learning how to give compelling responses can be a real boon to your facilitation toolkit.

Eloquent answers come from preparing a list of stories

You may have seen speakers who seem able to immediately respond to every question with an elaborate, subtle, insightful, and entertaining answer. The speaker never stumbles or gets off-track. And you might then compare their performance to your own inarticulate, stuttering replies and wonder whether you're just *missing* something. But it turns out, there's a trick.

Some years ago, I ended up inadvertently following one of my intellectual heroes from conference to conference, listening to him speak and answer questions at each. At the first event, I thought he was the smartest and most articulate human I had ever seen. At the second, I wondered why he was repeating himself so much. And by the third event, I got it.

The "trick" is to write down a list of powerful stories from your own life and experiences which are relevant to your field: unusual case studies, humorous anecdotes, adventurous struggles, personal blunders and triumphs, etc. And then, when someone asks you a question, you simply riffle through this mental file, extract the most relevant entry, and deploy it in all its glory.

If you're having trouble dredging your life for memories, it's helpful to grab a notebook and walk through each of your life's major threads—personal, social, professional, geographic—from start to finish. Throughout each, you'll find a few major "anchor memories" which you can mentally explore around to recover other forgotten fragments. Then repeat the process, but with an eye toward the second-hand experiences of the friends and colleagues you've met along the way. You shouldn't take credit for other people's experiences or ideas, but you can certainly use them with attribution.

If you're teaching complete beginners, then you can get away with "borrowing" your stories from popular books and blogs and other people's presentations. But as an audience becomes more sophisticated, they're increasingly likely to have heard those famous stories before and are unlikely to be overly impressed by your retelling. Delivering a relevant and insightful story of your own, on the other hand, can surprise and delight even the most jaded of attendees.

Questions you choose not to answer

You aren't required to answer every question. If it's off-topic, overly specific, or out of scope, then you're allowed to say something like:

> *"That's a fair question, but it's a bit specific (and/or out of scope) for what we're talking about today. I'd be glad to chat about it after the event, if you don't need to rush off."*

If it's about something you were already planning on talking about later, then you can say:

> *"That's an excellent question and is something we're going to be talking about at length in about 20 minutes from now. So let me delay answering until then, and please remind me if I don't manage to get into it in enough detail."*

Or if you're simply out of time:

> *"I'd love to keep talking about this stuff, but we need to charge onwards if we're going to get through everything and get you guys out of here on time."*

Or if they're being highly contentious and won't let you move past a point they disagree with (usually around some loaded political issue):

> *"I can see we've got different takes on this one, which is fine, and it would probably be fun to thrash it out at length over a couple of pints. But for the sake of the timetable and the rest of the class, I'm going to have to just skip ahead and move on."*

If they *still* try to get in the last word, just give a sort of helpless shrug—as if to imply that you've already said all there is to say—and then continue with your teaching. Trying to explicitly acknowledge their ongoing objections (or to "win" the debate) is a trap which only succeeds in empowering them to prevent you from continuing.

Refusing to answer questions is an important tool for staying on schedule. You shouldn't refuse to answer *every* question, obviously, but you'll always need to draw the line somewhere if you intend to hit your timings.

Questions you are unable to answer

When asked something you simply don't know the answer to, it's usually better to admit your ignorance than to try bluffing your way through it. Audiences are impeccable bullshit detectors and trying to sneak one past them is a surefire way of burning your goodwill and credibility.

If it's simply a difficult question with no clear "best" answer, then you can return to your story archive:

> *"To be honest, I've never found a satisfying and convincing best answer here. One way I've seen a few smart people approach it is to... [Switch into story-telling mode to give them an example even if it isn't a definitive answer.]"*

If you're asked to answer something that you really *should* know, then you can fess up to it while also promising to find out for them:

"You know what, I actually have no idea, and I really should. Let me research that during the next break and report back on what I discover."

If the question is important to a large percentage of the audience, but can't be quickly researched, then you can assign it to yourself as homework:

"I don't know, but I think I know someone who will. Let me ask around a bit after the workshop and try to dig up an answer, and I'll send what I learn to you all along with the workshop materials and slides. Sound good?"

Or if it's something which is wildly specific, obscure, and not something anybody would expect you to know:

"I truly don't have even the foggiest idea. Does anyone else happen to have any experience with that one?"

The attendees probably already understand that a) you're not omniscient and 2) the workshop's duration is finite. As such, they tend not to be overly intransigent about expecting you to answer every single question.

Lessons learned:

- Eloquent answers come from preparing a list of potentially relevant stories
- You don't have to answer every question

How to recover the crowd after an exercise

The class has just finished a fun, high-energy exercise, and you now need to recover their attention and get them listening to you again. But they're still engaged in the exercise, and they're talking, and some of them are either unwilling or unable to hear you. What to do?

As a bit of warning: I'm going to ask you to do something which will feel very strange and counterintuitive. It turns out that the best way to recover a rowdy crowd is to get going *before* everyone is paying attention. This means you're going to have to talk over people, and they're potentially going to keep ignoring you. At least for a bit. But I promise that these approaches work and—once you've gotten over the awkward feeling—they're the easiest, most widely applicable solution to the issue.

Before we look at the solutions, I want to highlight the *wrong* approach, which is to use your authority as a crutch, standing at the front of the room and demanding that people be quiet before you continue. This is a bad fit for workshops where you're dealing with (mostly) adults who (mostly) want to be there. The issue is that most of the class will immediately give you their attention as soon as you call for it. Using your authority to strongarm the entire audience makes you seem hostile toward the ones who have already done what you asked.

A better solution—assuming you can't just go individual—is to use a bit of facilitation judo to turn the crowd's momentum against itself. Let's look at two ways to make that happen: talking in circles and borrowing goodwill.

Talking in circles

Imagine that you've called the end of an exercise. Four of the six groups are now paying attention, whereas the other two groups remain distracted.

My favorite solution is to "talk in circles", which means that you begin lecturing at normal volume, in your normal position, but without saying anything important. It's like being a lawyer or politician: lots of words, no content.

Before long, people will realize they're missing out and start tuning in, without you ever needing to demand it. And if they don't, the rest of the class will soon become annoyed at the chatter, bringing them into line through a bit of gentle shushing.

Your attention-gathering monologue might sound something like this:

> *"As I'm sure you found, there are a lot of interesting points to discuss about this stuff, and lots of different opinions. And some of you probably felt that it was a little bit weird to talk about. The mistake people normally make is to get too stuck in the details and worry*

too much about doing everything perfectly instead of just getting it done. My first experience with this was a few years ago when [on-topic but largely unimportant anecdote]..."

This example is so incredibly *vacuous* that it's painful to write. Which is sort of the point. Perhaps it reminds you of some recent presidential speeches. It is totally devoid of any actual information, but it is just going in circles around the topic.

Within a minute or so, you've got the whole crowd's attention without ever needing to pick a fight or cause a scene.

Borrowing goodwill

The second strategy works similarly, but instead of expecting distracted participants to pay attention to *you*, you're setting them up to pay attention to one of their *peers*. It works by recognizing that although *some* of the class is distracted, others are paying attention. And by asking someone who *is* paying attention to do a "stand and share", you gain the moral authority to firmly cut off anyone still talking over them. After all, they're now being rude to one of their peers.

Using *your own* authority to bring attention back to *yourself* is a dangerous gambit; people will obey, but they aren't happy to be made to feel like a child while doing so. But interestingly, using your authority to demand attention for *someone else* has all the same benefits, with none of the downsides. "Please be quiet, you're being rude to *me*," carries a totally different emotional payload from, "Please be quiet, you're being rude to *Jessica*."

To put it into practice, start by picking a "volunteer" who is both paying attention and sitting near to you.

If you don't already know their name, ask them to remind you. You can do this in a normal speaking voice, since this exchange feels more like a "side conversation" than a part of the core lecture.

Once you've got their name, ask them an extremely directed question, just like at the end of any small group exercise. "Jessica, would you mind standing up and sharing how you were thinking about X, and what result you got?" Your volunteer will stand up, and then likely stumble since people aren't used to speaking to a group who aren't fully attentive. That's fine.

This next bit is the crux of the facilitation. Tell Jessica not to worry. Tell her to just ignore the other folks and start talking anyway. The pieces are now all in play, and this is your moment to (benevolently) seize control.

From the instant your volunteer stands up and attempts to speak—even if they only manage a single word—you gain the moral permission to strong-arm everyone else into listening to them, loudly saying something like, "Hey, everyone, Jessica has the stage, pay attention for a minute please." And they'll glance up, see that she's already standing (and looking slightly uncomfortable), and immediately pay attention.

Even if you need to yell it rather loudly and directly, the situation you've constructed means that the other students will feel like your behavior is completely justified. In fact they'll feel that they themselves have made the blunder by talking over one of their peers. They'll give their attention to the speaker, and you can easily reclaim it afterwards now that everyone is calm.

This sounds fairly elaborate, but in practice it only takes 10 seconds. Call the end of the exercise, get a volunteer, learn their name, prompt them to stand up and start talking, and then cut off the rest of the crowd, allow the volunteer to finish, and continue from there.

The post-coffee battleground

Amusingly, the mundane task of recovering your audience from a coffee break is one of the most complicated facilitation challenges you'll ever face. And it's important; if you regularly require an extra 5 or 10 minutes to recover your crowd from breaks, then your full-day workshops will reliably run 15 or 30 minutes late, which is no good at all. In an ideal world, helper staff would corral the crowd on your behalf. But in practice, you'll rarely get so lucky.

Let's say that your audience is on a well-deserved coffee break. They're having fun and mingling. In some ways, it's what they came for! You've given them 15 minutes and it's time to get going again.

The way it typically works it that you yell a three-minute warning, and nobody moves. And then you give them the one-minute warning. And the zero-minute deadline. But they're still having a grand old chat and you're starting to look like the wild-haired old man in the square, yelling at pigeons.

The solution is a combination of setting expectations, going individual, talking in circles, and borrowing goodwill. Yep, we're using all of it.

Before the break, **set expectations**. I like to say:

> *"We've got 15 minutes for coffee. It's [wherever]. I'll come by to give you guys a 3-minute warning, and then when [start time] arrives, I'm going to start talking, even if nobody is in the room. All right, go for it."*

Before the time hits, I make the three-minute warning to the group, and then also spend the next two minutes wandering through and **going individual**. Yelling at pigeons never works. But you *can* get them to move by walking up and individually asking them to take the conversation back to their seats. As long as some portion are in the room when you begin talking, it's enough.

At the very moment that the break time has finished, **begin talking in circles.** Not saying anything critical, but standing on stage and looking for all the world like you don't give a damn that half the audience is missing. Proceed as if you're completely indifferent that those seats are empty. Just get going.

After a minute, if the missing folks still haven't rushed in due to their fear of missing out, **borrow someone's credibility** by singling someone out who is near to the break area and saying:

"Hey, would you mind popping into the other room (or wherever the break area is) and letting them know we've started?"

They'll rush off, worried that they're about to miss some crucial nugget of wisdom, and their urgency will spread to the folks who they're asking to come join the group. It works quickly.

Having done all this, if a few people *still* don't come through, I just assume they're doing something important like falling in love or securing a business partner, and I leave them to it.

Never single people out or harass them for being late; that's treating them like children and doesn't help. Just keep to the schedule, charge on with your material, and let them decide for themselves that they don't want to risk missing anything again.

For full-day events, expect to repeat the above steps after every break (so usually three times in a day, twice for coffee and once for lunch). On the bright side, it does get significantly easier each time as the audience learns what to expect.

Once you've honored your schedule in this way on the first break, you'll have trained the attendees that if they aren't in their seats on time, you're starting without them. They won't realize that you were talking in circles, so loss aversion will get them to show up on time in the future.

Yeah, that sounds like a lot of work. And to be honest, it is. It's a task outside of teaching which requires a fair amount of energy and attention. It means your breaks are always five minutes shorter than they should be, since you're spending those final minutes wrangling folks back into their seats. But it's a crucial endeavor if you want any hope of keeping to the schedule and finishing on time.

Lessons learned:

- To quickly recover distracted participants, you can "talk in circles" by speaking at a normal volume without saying anything important
- Alternately, you can "borrow goodwill" by prompting a student to stand and share, and then asking everyone else to pay attention to them
- To be able to start on time after a break, expect to spend the last 5 minutes of your break getting folks back into their seats

Overcoming hostility, skepticism, and troublemakers

One of the toughest gigs I ever taught was an executive education workshop for a multi-billion euro German company which had just suffered a hostile takeover at the hands of a private equity firm. The new owners wanted to "shake things up", so they'd hired me (through a middleman) to run a day-long session on how modern startups innovate. Hoo boy. My audience consisted of thirty C-level executives who had been pulled away from their departments and forced (by their new, unwelcome boss) to sit in a conference room all day listening to some American kid talk about companies so small that the revenue wouldn't even be a blip on their radar. Needless to say, they were not pleased.

By 10am I was hearing some grumbling, and by noon I was facing a full-blown mutiny: they refused to speak in English, ignored my existence, took out their computers, and got back to work on their day jobs. I was saved by the bell when lunch began, which gave us all some breathing room. And even more fortunately, I happened to be co-teaching alongside a native German speaker, Andreas, who used the lunch break to masterfully demonstrate how to disarm both a hostile crowd and hostile individuals. And while I wouldn't claim that it ended up being my best workshop ever, I *can* claim that it at least succeeded, despite impossible odds. Following the emergency intervention, everyone returned after lunch (which was a miracle on its own), they participated, and they left satisfied.

Sometimes the whole room is against you before you even start talking. Other times, one particularly irksome individual makes it his or her mission to ruin your day. But as scary as it might seem, you can almost always find a way to calm a hostile attendee, so long as you're able to identify what's gone wrong.

Here's a handy reference, and then we'll get into the details:

What's the trouble?	How to handle it
The context: The whole audience doesn't want to be there (usually because someone forced them), or they're frustrated by bad logistics earlier in the day	Explicitly acknowledge their concerns with a minimal intro, and then skip straight to delivering major value
The bore: One person has an endless stream of incredibly specific questions that are irrelevant to the bulk of your audience	Suggest that you need to spend some time talking 1-on-1 to solve those issues and ask them to come find you after the workshop or during a break; use this future conversation as an excuse to deflect all their further questions
The isolationist: Someone is refusing to engage in the exercises and just seems zoned out	Figure out whether they're just a spectator, or whether they're shy and afraid of engaging with the other attendees, and then help appropriately
The expert: One person knows it all already, feels like the material is beneath them, and is either quietly hostile or actively undermining you	Put them on a pedestal by including them in the teaching as an expert and asking for their opinion and experiences whenever possible

The trouble-maker: One person is being enormously disruptive and you can't find a way to calm them	Call an early coffee break and talk to them 1-on-1 to understand (and hopefully solve) their concerns. If needed, suggest that the workshop isn't for them, offer a full refund, and politely ask them to leave
The mystery: You aren't sure what's gone wrong, but the group just doesn't seem to be happy with something	Work the crowd during the next break, where you can talk to them human-to-human instead of teacher-to-student, and try to understand their concerns and objections

Exciting, right? All the fun of being a hostage negotiator, but without the risk of getting shot.

Hostile crowds who don't want to be there (acknowledge it)

The most common reason for initial grumpiness among participants is that someone else (their boss, their spouse, their parents, a judge) has forced them to attend. And doubly so if they feel your workshop is beneath them. Plus, everyone is busy. This all combines to make them skeptical about the value of spending time in the workshop. So they show up grumbling and with their phones in hand, ready to distract themselves with email.

Just like when giving a good intro, the general strategy for a hostile crowd is to explicitly acknowledge their top concern and then find the fastest way possible to start delivering major value.

For example, if they're extremely busy and have been forced to be there, you might acknowledge it by saying:

> *"I know you're all are super busy. If you need to step out to answer an email or take a call or anything else, please feel free to do so. I won't be offended. We all understand that stuff can come up suddenly sometimes."*

Almost nobody will take you up on this offer unless there's an actual emergency, in which case they would have stepped out anyway. But by saying it (and meaning it), you've shown that you understand and respect their concerns, which suggests that you value their time as highly as they do. It also gives them an escape hatch, so they're able to stop stressing about the possibility of being trapped if something comes up.

Let's pick up the narrative of my near-disastrous German workshop. After doing some lunchtime reconnaissance to figure out the nature of the problem, Andreas disarmed most of the hostility by saying something like this:

> *"Look, we certainly can't understand your businesses as well as you already do, and there's no way we're going to be able to figure out—in one day—how to solve the problems that you've been wrestling with for ages. But startups keep popping out of nowhere and messing with your market, right? And we do understand how they think and how they work. So our hope is that if you'll let*

us share that with you, then maybe it will lead you to some helpful thoughts and ideas further down the line."

Simply saying out loud what they were already thinking (that we couldn't possibly understand and solve their problems) got maybe 25 out of the 30 back onto our side. But there were still five hostile individuals. Fear not: we'll return to them in a moment. So that's the first step of acknowledging their concerns. Once you've done that, follow it up by immediately delivering some major value.

Incidentally, this is also how I position myself when I'm brought in to teach a crowd of experts who are more successful, powerful, rich, and generally better at life than me. The general pattern is to acknowledge, reframe, and scope down:

1. **Acknowledge:** "You guys are obviously miles ahead of me in your lives/careers/businesses and have a ton of stuff going on that I wouldn't even know where to start with..."
2. **Reframe:** "...So I'm not here to try to solve all your problems or to tell you what to do."
3. **Scope down to an area where you can add clear value:** "But I've been obsessing over the question of X, and I'm hoping that if you'll let me share the theory/skills/thinking/examples/etc., that you'll be able to find a couple useful tools to bring back to your own worlds."

Once you've finished this brief acknowledgement of their concerns, skip ahead to delivering real value as quickly as possible.

Oblivious individuals (sideline them)

Counter-intuitively, dealing with a single difficult individual can be considerably tougher than dealing with a whole crowd.

The most common type of disruptive individual isn't actively *hostile* but is just a bit oblivious to social cues. As such, they're asking an unending stream of questions which are irrelevant for the bulk of your attendees. Whether they're hogging attention with self-promotional "questions" or are just a bit long-winded and off-topic, your response can be the same. Interrupt them and say:

> *"Let me jump in here for a second. This sounds like a pretty specific issue. Let's find some time to chat 1-on-1 about that during the next break so I can properly help you. Cool? (Then, speaking to the class) "Okay, does anyone have any other questions?"*

And then move on to the next person. If they ask more questions, you can just deflect it to your future 1-on-1.

Now, I want to clarify that sidelining someone in this way does *not* involve attacking them, belittling them, being rude to them, or in any way making them feel bad. And you don't need to raise your voice. (Yelling over one person feels extremely aggressive.) They often care *a lot* about what you're teaching, which is why they keep trying to ask these bizarre questions. So you aren't forgetting about them or ignoring them — you're just moving their questions from the workshop itself (where the questions don't fit) to a 1-on-1 conversation (where their questions fit brilliantly). And of course, if you use this tactic during your session, be sure to track them down and help them out during the next available break.

Disengaged and non-participating attendees (Ignore or wingman)

You'll sometimes have one or two people sitting off to the side who are refusing to participate in exercises and who basically seem emotionally clocked out. They'll pay quiet attention during lectures and then, when it's time for any sort of exercise, will retreat into their phone or computer.

This tends to drive new facilitators crazy. They'll blame either the student ("Why won't they just participate!?") or themselves ("Why couldn't I make it more interesting!?") and will sometimes make a scene of pushing the outsider to get involved (which can backfire horribly for reasons that will soon become apparent).

There are two very legitimate reasons why individuals might choose to isolate themselves:

1. They're actually a spectator rather than a participant, so they're politely staying quiet and out of the way
2. They feel confused, overwhelmed, shy, or intimidated, and find it emotionally difficult to engage with the other attendees who all seem more capable and confident

When you see someone who is disengaged, your first task is to figure out if one of these two causes is behind it. I like to wander over and say hello during the next exercise or break.

"Hey, how's it going? Just wanted to check in on how you're doing. Seems like this workshop isn't for you... would you mind sharing what you were hoping to get out of attending?"

And sometimes they'll say, "Oh, yeah, I've been doing this stuff for 20 years and don't want to meddle with the folks you're teaching, but I was curious to see how you run the session. Is that okay?" In which case, great, they're just not a participant and you can sort of leave them in the corner and ignore them. Or they might say, "Oh, I just started working for the venue and they asked me to come sit in on an event to get a better sense of how everything works." Again, they're just a spectator, not a participant, and you can happily ignore them. Or maybe they say, "We're in the middle of a crisis at work and I really wanted to attend, but I also need to keep sending emergency emails and didn't want to be a distraction to the other attendees." Neat, that's thoughtful of them.

In these cases, just let them be. After all, they're adults. However, I do generally ask them to move to a seat which is physically separate from the other attendees (if they haven't already done so). Otherwise, their non-participation can mess with the groupwork of whoever they're sitting with.

However, you need to take a totally different approach when someone has isolated themselves due to shyness, fear, or confusion. They'll often have taken a solitary seat, away from the other attendees, physically separating themselves to avoid whatever awkwardness they fear.

As the facilitator, you are the wingman for your shy and overwhelmed attendees. When someone is alone—but still secretly wants to be involved—you need to (very gently) overrule their comfort zone and do as much as humanly possible to clear the air of awkwardness and place them into an accepting group. If they're physically isolated, this will involve saying hello, learning their name, chatting with them until they're comfortable, having them stand up with you, walking with them to a new group, and telling the new group that they're lucky to have a new member named Wilbur (or whatever). And then stay with them until you see that the dynamic is working and that your lost sheep has been fully included.

If the group is excluding their new member (which can happen simply because they've already got momentum), interrupt them by saying something like, "Hey guys, Wilbur is on your team, don't throw away the advantage of an extra brain! Catch him up with what you're working on and get him involved!" It's your job to make the space.

(This is also, incidentally, how you find a place for attendees who have arrived late, in the middle of an exercise.)

I sometimes see facilitators try to wingman, but they don't take it far enough. Encouraging a shy individual to get involved will **not** be sufficient. The job isn't finished yet! The scary part is in approaching a group of strangers and breaching the conversation. *That's* the bit you need to help with, and it's why you need to get their name, physically travel with them to the new group, ensure they have a chair, introduce them in both directions, and stick around until they've been fully accepted. But remember that you need to chat to them and figure out what's going on first; marching someone around the room before understanding their motivation for being alone is a recipe for embarrassing yourself.

So, when you see someone failing to engage, first work to figure out whether they're a spectator (in which case you can just leave them be) or whether they're shy/overwhelmed/scared (in which case you wingman them into a welcoming group).

Hostile individuals (put them on a pedestal)

Actively hostile individuals are the toughest nut to crack, since they require a combination of networking (to figure out what they're unhappy about) plus delicate facilitation. But solving this problem is still very doable and is vastly preferred over letting a hostile agent tear apart your workshop from the inside out.

The crucial realization is that individuals are almost always hostile because they already have a bunch of experience with what you're teaching and think you're talking down to them or undermining their position as the expert. You solve this by putting them on a pedestal, highlighting their expertise, and repeatedly asking for their opinion.

At the German workshop, the CTO was hugely hostile, and was speaking up to contradict and undermine basically everything we said. We were claiming that startups succeed, at least in part, due to their ability to quickly iterate, whereas the company in attendance took six months to make even small changes. But that's understandable! After all, they had billions in revenue and couldn't afford even a tiny security breach. Still, the CTO worried he would be fired for being too "slow" compared to the examples we were sharing. During lunch, Andreas sat individually with each of the hostile individuals to learn their names, ask about their concerns, and show them that we were listening. For the

CTO, we used the standard solution of putting him on a pedestal. We set him up like this:

> "Startups have this massive advantage of being able to iterate quickly on their product, tech, and marketing. But of course, they can afford to be fast and loose since they don't have an existing customer base, brand, or revenue to worry about.
>
> "This obviously changes as you get bigger. [Mr. CTO], would you mind taking a couple minutes to tell us about the places where this sort of approach would and wouldn't work for your company, and whether there are any ways to get some of the benefits without compromising security and reputation? I know there's a ton to say about this, but you've only got three minutes, so be quick!"

Boom. Just like that, he's our biggest fan. From then on, instead of slapping down everything we said, he was actively participating and looking for ways to adapt our message to their context. He even went so far as to jump to our defense later in the day when someone else raised an objection. After all, we'd put him in a place of honor in front of his entire executive team.

In general, the disarmament process is:

1. Discover that a hostile participant is lurking (this often requires talking to people before the event and during breaks)
2. Talk with them 1-on-1 during to learn their name and expertise (or whatever other objections they have)
3. Put them on a pedestal and bring them to your side by including them as an authority in your teaching

The expert's whole issue is that they feel like they have as much (or more) right to be teaching this material as you do. Disarm them by putting them on a pedestal and including them in your teaching as someone the rest of the class should look up to.

Although pre-event chit-chat can be draining, I always try to show up early and partake, since it's the best way to spot potential hostiles. The standard line of questioning is to simply try and get a sense of their expectations and goals:

> *"Hey, good to meet you. Mind if I ask why you showed up today? What are you hoping to get out of it?"*

This is an easy conversation starter for anyone at the workshop, and it *also* helps scan for a wide range of potential problems. Most folks will respond happily, and you can move on to say hello to someone else. But if you notice some skepticism, you can ask a bit more to check for expertise and other potential objections:

> *"Have you done this sort of stuff before...? Interesting, tell me more about that... Sounds like you're pretty expert at all this, may I ask how you ended up here today?"*

It should sound like you're making small talk, even though you're really trying to identify the experts (and anyone else who doesn't want to be there). Then, later in your session, you can do this bit of facilitation judo to instantly transform a detractor into a supporter:

> *"You all know this stuff, of course. I was talking to Jamie earlier and it sounded like their team is pretty much nailing it. Jamie, do you mind sharing your approach real quick?"*

Or when someone from the room asks you a question, you can redirect it to your (formerly) hostile friend:

> *"Hmm, great question. Abigail, how does your team deal with that one?"*

People find it extremely difficult to continue being hostile after you've put them on a pedestal. If you've got multiple experts in the room, you can start running whole lecture sections as a facilitated conversation and/or interview. After one of your newfound experts has offered their perspective, you can follow up by checking in from anyone else who might also have their own experience, like this:

> *"Nice, that's a perfect approach for that situation. Does anyone handle it differently? Or has anyone seen cases where this approach doesn't apply?"*

Sometimes your attendees will disagree with each other, or you'll disagree with all of them. But that's not so much of a powder keg as you might suspect. Consider the expert panelists on a talk show or conference stage: they're all happy to have their voices heard, even if the other panelists (or the host) disagree on the matter at hand. Although you shouldn't make them feel a fool, you can certainly contradict or disagree with them, springboarding off their answer with your own perspective:

> *"The approach Jake just shared has been industry standard for years. A ton of great companies have become hugely successful with it and still use it to this day. But some of the fastest-growing recent startups have chosen to shake it up and do things very differently, largely due to running into problems when X happens. What*

they're doing now is super interesting, and completely backwards from the conventional wisdom..."

Or even more bluntly:

"So that's obviously a solid approach since it's been working, and Famous Person X has said that they do it the same way. But I prefer to do, well, pretty much exactly the opposite. Let me talk through how I've been thinking about it recently, and maybe you'll find it useful to have both options in your toolkit."

Often the expert is giving a correct answer, but for a different (or more specific) scenario than the workshop is actually about. In this case, you can simply clarify the scope:

"Yes, that's absolutely the right financial advice for someone in situation X, and it sounds like Laura is an expert on that, so if anyone has questions, I'd encourage you to find her during the break to chat or grab her email. But today we're talking mainly about situation Y, which behaves rather differently."

Yes, the wordplay is a bit delicate. But it's handled successfully every day by talk show hosts and panel moderators. In fact, if you've ever presided over an ego-heavy meeting, then this is something you already know how to do. And, if not, it's a very learnable skill.

The hostiles won't always make themselves known during pre-event networking. If you see someone looking skeptical or grumpy about what you're saying while teaching, it's a sign that they might be a lurking hostile. In this case, you can try to pull the objection out of them so you can deal with it:

"You look a bit suspicious about what I just said. Have you had different experiences, or maybe come across situations where this doesn't work so well?"

You certainly aren't required to draw out their concerns like this and might prefer to just let them quietly simmer. But if you like getting the objections out in the open, a line like the above will generally start the discussion, and you can then put them on a pedestal, include them as an expert, and continue from there.

The nuclear option

If someone is being *hugely* disruptive and can't be placated in any of the ways already discussed, it can be worth calling an early coffee break just to talk to them 1-on-1. This is obviously problematic for your schedule but is still sometimes better than letting them continue to run amok. In other cases, you can ride out the problem until the next scheduled break and deal with them then.

Sometimes you'll identify a solution to the unruly attendee's problem and can successfully appease them. In other cases, they're just going to make more trouble no matter what you do. If folks bought tickets from you directly, you can pull the troublemaker aside to somewhere private, observe that workshop doesn't seem to be a good fit, offer your apologies, give a full refund, and see them out. (If you're teaching a corporate or client gig you won't always have this option and may just have to deal with them.)

Now, I know you'd like to be "peaceful" and "patient" and hope that it "works itself out". But in this situation, you can't. By being "kind" to one troublemaker, you're favoring their disruptions over the legitimate needs of everyone else in the room. A bunch of people have shown up to try and learn something, and it's your obligation to obliterate anything that stands in their way.

Of course, you still need to be polite while doing so. That's what the apology and the refund are for. In one extreme case, I actually paid for a cab to take an especially toxic person all the way home, in *addition* to a full refund. Despite the fact that they were the bane of my existence on that particular day, I humbled myself before them:

> "I'm so sorry that I promoted this workshop so sloppily and made it sound like something it's not. I really hate to have dragged you all the way across town for nothing. Here, let me refund the ticket and give you money for a cab. No, please, I insist. It's the least I can do after inconveniencing you so terribly. I'm really sorry. Let me walk you out.

Sounds a bit over the top, but they left without causing a scene. And my other students deserved it.

As a final reminder, I'd like to emphasize that most attendees are lovely, and they want you to succeed. This stuff doesn't come up too often, but it's good to know how to handle it when it does.

Lessons learned:

- For hostile crowds, acknowledge their top concern then skip ahead to delivering value
- For oblivious individuals with irrelevant or overly specific questions, sideline them and then chat 1-on-1 with them later

- For disengaged individuals, figure out if they're a spectator or are marginalized, and then either ignore them or wingman them
- For hostile experts, put them on a pedestal and include them as an authority in your teaching
- For implacable and highly disruptive individuals, talk to them 1-on-1, give them a full refund, and ask them to leave

Staying on schedule and dealing with delays

It's amazing how rarely facilitators keep to their schedule. Running a slipped schedule is a massive and unnecessary drain on both goodwill and energy.

There are a few pieces to handle properly:

1. **Keeping your own time** by using two clocks
2. **Starting late** without frustrating the folks who are already there
3. **Recovering lost time**
4. **Running late** without frustrating the folks who need to leave

Keep time by using two clocks

To stay on schedule, you'll need two clocks: a section timer and an exercise timer.

The section timer offers an at-a-glance reminder of how much time is remaining until the next break or big switch in topic. It's ideally a countdown (i.e. "22 minutes remaining") instead of an actual clock (i.e. "it's currently 4:13 and this section ends at 4:45, which means I've got..."), since the latter slows you down and allows for errors. Any timer is fine, so long as it's quick to read and quick to set. I use a €5 kitchen timer which looks like this:

Importantly, this timer is not allowed to be your phone. Consider the negative impact of having dinner with someone who keeps glancing at their phone... Holding and checking your phone projects massive disinterest in your audience, even if it was for a workshop-relevant reason. (If you're caught unprepared and *must* use your phone, keep it flat on the podium with the settings modified to never turn off the screen or lock itself, which allows you to quickly glance at it without touching it and without the phone being seen by the audience.)

As a section starts, check the finishing time on your Skeleton, do your mental math once about how much time you have available, set your countdown timer, and leave it somewhere on a table or floor where you can keep an eye on it.

The purpose is to warn you, as soon as is possible, that you're starting to run behind. The earlier you catch it, the easier it is to get back on track. If you're caught with only a wristwatch, you can create a makeshift countdown timer by putting a small mark (with either a whiteboard marker or a bit of a sticky note's sticky strip) where the minute-hand will end up after this section is over. Some slide clickers have a built-in section timer, although they generally require some extra software. Most slide software will offer a timer while you're in presenter mode, but since it's not always easy to see your own screen, it's wise to bring a standalone solution.

The other clock, your exercise timer, is used to track the minutes of an exercise (e.g. five-minutes of small group discussion). Some facilitators put a timer up for everyone to see on the projector screen, but I believe it's more important to continue showing the exercise's prompt and instructions. Attendees have the memory of goldfish when it comes to task instructions.

Using your phone as a timer here is less of a problem, because the students are busy working while you're interacting with it. (If you're using the phone, start the exercise first, and *then* start the timer on your phone. This prevents you from looking at your phone while the students are looking at you.) A cheap stopwatch also works nicely. It doesn't matter whether the timer counts up or down, and it doesn't matter whether it has an alarm. Because often, you're going to choose to ignore it.

In most cases, exercise timings are more of a guideline than a strict rule. You might tell everyone that they have three minutes, but then, while walking the room and listening to them work, you realize that it's actually a hugely valuable and engaging task for everyone in attendance. Great! Let them have a couple extra minutes. You don't need to alert them about the change; just overrule the timer and roll with it. Once you start to hear groups drifting into silence or getting off-topic, then you know it's time to wrap up and move on. (I'd never let a conversation drag on for 10 minutes, but adding or removing one or two minutes is extremely common.)

As such, the audience doesn't necessarily need to see the timer. Instead, give them verbal reminders about how close they are to the end:

> "Alright, you have five minutes, get to work... This is the half-way mark, two and a half minutes remaining... One minute to go, get those final thoughts down... Thirty seconds left... Ten seconds... Five, four, three, two, one, time!!!"

A verbal countdown lets you creatively adjust the precise timings without anyone noticing the difference. Everyone confused? Allow yourself some time to go individual with each group and answer questions by lengthening the exercise. Folks starting to take out their phones or talk about weekend plans? Maybe this discussion topic isn't as riveting as you had hoped, and you should call the end of the exercise immediately instead of waiting for the timer to run down.

Of course, just because no matter how well you keep your own time, things can still slip out of control for reasons largely beyond your control. And the correct reaction to that common conundrum can make a world of difference.

Announce late starts as soon as you know about them

Nobody minds waiting. But everybody hates waiting if they don't know how long they're waiting for. So as soon as you know you're going to be starting late, you should let folks know:

> *"Hey everyone, welcome. Looks like a fair number of people are stuck in traffic, so we're going to push back the start time by 15 minutes to 9:15, at which point we'll start promptly. We had a bit of flex in the schedule, so we'll still aim to finish at the scheduled time. There's plenty of coffee and snacks in the back, so please grab some refreshments, make yourself at home, and say hello to each other. Let me know if you have any questions."*

Be specific about the new start time. Don't just say you'll be "starting soon" or in "about five minutes". Set clear expectations.

If more folks are wandering in, just walk over and tell them the new plan as they arrive. If it's too big of a crowd to go individual, just re-make the announcement every few minutes.

Once you've announced a new start time, *honor it*. Even if the crowd is smaller than you'd like, your hands are now tied and you've got to make the best of whoever happens to be in the room. You're allowed to delay the start time exactly once. Doing so repeatedly will obliterate your credibility.

Recover time by cutting content

Instead of running late, it's generally preferred to get back on track by cutting content. These cuts can be difficult, but it's best to make them decisively as soon as you notice you've fallen behind. Otherwise you end up talking too fast (bad for learning), compromising your breaks (bad for energy), and *still* ending late (bad for everything).

The best case is to have already included flexible spring sections which are easy to delete or reduce (such as Q&A). In this case, you can simply use them for their intended purpose of getting you back on schedule. This is a perfect option and should be your go-to whenever possible. It's seamless, painless, and leaves your schedule and energy levels intact.

If you don't have springs (or are further behind than your springs can handle), then you'll need to start deleting important stuff. This is painful. To recover five minutes, you can delete an anecdote or example or the discussion section after an exercise. To recover 10-15 minutes, you can delete a whole exercise. To recover 20-30 minutes, you can delete an entire Learning Outcome.

It's tempting to try to "get through everything" by leaving the lectures in place and just deleting all the exercises. This sounds good on paper, but essentially undoes all your hard work of designing a high-energy and engaging workshop, degrading it into a long, dry lecture. Better, in my experience, to cut a whole section and do a good job teaching what's left instead of a bad job teaching everything.

Run long by asking for permission and creating a safety net

The main benefit of finishing on time is that almost no facilitators manage to do it. So when you do, the audience is *delighted*. It's an easy way to end on a high note, dramatically improving the perception (and feedback score) of your entire session.

That being said, sometimes you're going to run long. It's not a big deal. But also, sometimes your attendees won't be able to stay. And since running long is ultimately your responsibility, you need to make them feel like they've gotten everything they showed up for. You do that by reassuring them, *in advance*, that they aren't going to miss anything, since you're going to do the extra work to provide it to them remotely. This is called "creating a safety net".

The announcement sounds like this:

Telling them: *"Hey everyone, it looks like we're about 45 minutes behind, which puts us on track to end at 1645 instead of 1600."*

Checking for impact: *"I know some of you have stuff you need to get to. Can I get a quick raise of hands of who needs to run off at 1600? Okay... And who would be able to stick around a bit longer?"*

Telling them (continued): *"Alright, so if it's okay, we're going to run long. If you need to leave early, don't worry about it at all, I understand. You can just step out whenever you need to."*

Creating a safety net: *"But I know you don't want to miss anything, so what I'm going to do is send everyone an email with a full write-up of all the stuff we talked about in the section you missed, which is going to be about [topic]. I'll also send you the slides, some recommended reading, and a couple exercises you can do to practice. And if you have any questions, please email or call me and I'll walk you through it."*

Asking permission: *"Does that sound okay for everyone?"*

The most important thing is to tell them, in advance, about the change in plans. People get *extremely* jittery if you're still in the middle of teaching as the clock is approaching the end of the workshop. And as you silently run over time, they'll be sitting there having an internal crisis, wondering if it's rude to sneak out or if you'll be done soon enough that they can stay and not miss anything.

Lessons learned:

- Keep track of time by using a countdown section timer (not your phone), plus a separate exercise timer (your phone is okay)
- If you're planning to start late you should proactively tell folks the new start time and then honor it
- Include some flexible Spring Sections to make it easier to recover time and finish on schedule
- If you do need to run late, create a safety net for folks who can't stay

Charisma can be manufactured with a clicker, a watch, and some small behaviors

Charisma acts as a multiplier to your skills by causing people to pay better attention and to give you more benefit of the doubt. In a workshop context, a bit of charisma causes goodwill and attention to stay higher for longer. So although it's not strictly necessary, it's certainly handy. Fortunately, it's fairly easy to boost your teaching charisma by changing a handful of small (but crucial) charisma-impacting behaviors.

To borrow the framework and language of Olivia Fox, author of *The Charisma Myth*,[17] coming across as "charismatic" is the result of projecting three qualities:

---

[17] As an introvert, I found *The Charisma Myth* both interesting and helpful. For our purposes here, it provides a helpful framework which leads to the set of actionable tips provided in this section. Her book is much more about charisma in day-to-day life, so I've tested and adapted it to get a workshop version.

- **Power** (authority, credibility)
- **Warmth** (friendliness, openness)
- **Presence** (the audience feels like you are undistracted and paying full attention to them)

You need all three. Having lots of power but a shortage of either warmth or presence, for example, will cause you to seem hostile or aloof, respectively.

Power is the easiest to get and maintain. In fact, you get it for free simply because you happen to be the person who is currently standing on stage and whose name is on the event blurb. Of course, it's possible to throw it away (for example by being far too self-deprecating in your intro, letting a hostile participant run all over you, or allowing the schedule to slip too far), but you always start with plenty. And by following the design and facilitation guidelines throughout this book, you'll hold on to what you started with.

Warmth and presence, on the other hand, must be actively fostered. It's easy though; all it takes is a clicker and a watch.

The single biggest improvement you can make is to get a clicker and stop standing in the stage's "charisma dead-zone", which is anywhere behind your laptop. Standing in the dead-zone an immediate and infallible way to *obliterate* both warmth and presence. This is partly due to your eyes being drawn to your screen instead of your audience, and partly due to the physical wall you've placed between yourself and your students.

To escape the dead zone, you just need to get a clicker and then stand in front of your computer instead of behind it. Don't rely on venues to provide a clicker — it's too important.

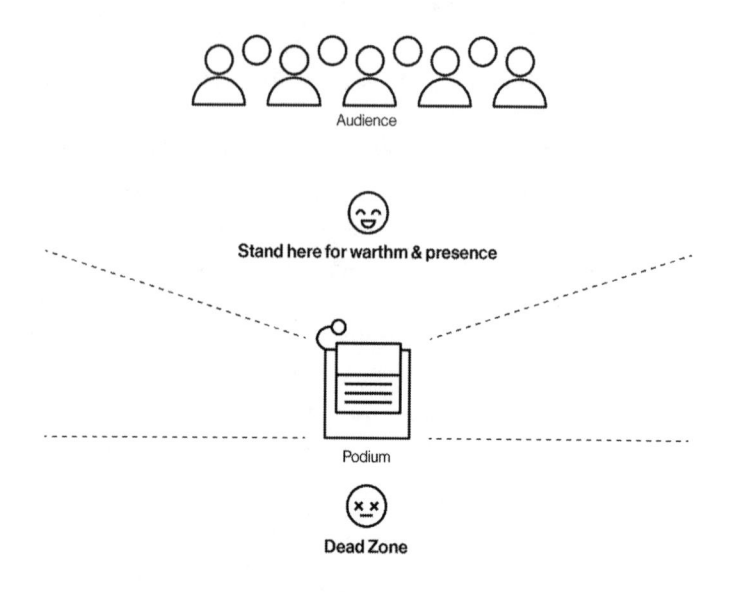

```
        Audience
   (smiley)
Stand here for warthm & presence

   [Podium]
   Podium

   (x_x)
   Dead Zone
```

Another big improvement is to **stop using your phone as a clock and timer.** We've already covered this in the previous section.

Thirdly, you should be walking the room during exercises, getting yourself away from the stage and among the audience. We've already discussed the educational benefits of this (earlier in Part 2, Walking the Room), but it also breaks down any barriers between you and the audience and makes you seem vastly more friendly and accessible.

Lastly, you want to limit behaviors which come across as defensive or jumpy. The biggest one is to rush to answer student questions before the student has finished asking them. Or alternately, to nod and gesture quickly and repeatedly throughout their entire question as if you just *can't wait* to answer with something oh so brilliant. Better, instead, to let them finish saying whatever they are going to say, pause for an additional moment or two (this beat of silence is powerful), and *then* respond.

Less critical, but also worth doing, is to work toward reducing your verbal and physical fidgets. The most common physical fidgets are pacing, crossing and uncrossing your arms or legs, and readjusting clothing that has ridden up or down. (I'm personally also terrible about playing with—and inevitably dropping—whatever I happen to be holding.) If you aren't sure about your fidgets, mix yourself a strong drink and then sit down to watch a video of yourself on stage. It's slightly horrifying to see all the things you're doing wrong but is invaluable for spotting (and then fixing) these sorts of behaviors.

As mentioned, charisma isn't strictly necessary, and you shouldn't worry too much if you've got a fidget (or whatever else) that you just can't seem to kick. But if you can change a couple small behaviors to get a little bit more charisma, I think you'll find yourself enjoying your new ability to engage a crowd. At the very least, buy yourself a clicker and stop standing in the dead-zone.

Lessons learned:

- Charisma is not a fundamental personality trait, but can be manufactured through behaviors which project and maintain warmth, attention, and power
- Buy a clicker and free yourself from the "charisma dead-zone" behind the podium
- Stop relying on your smartphone as a timer, and get an analog timer instead
- Walk the room during exercises and be fully present for your attendees

Protect your own energy by hiding during breaks

For events longer than a half-day, the facilitator's energy needs to be managed as carefully as the audience's. New facilitators *always* ignore this advice and run themselves ragged, especially if they're naturally outgoing and get a high from being on stage.

Teaching all day is exhausting. And this fatigue is not something to ignore and endure. Even if you feel okay, it's like staying up all night and then drinking 20 coffees: you're alert but stupid. And while *you* can't notice the difference, everyone else certainly can. Although most folks can credibly deliver a lecture while fatigued (albeit in a rambling fashion with a few too many tangents), they'll get significantly worse at empathizing and engaging with the audience, performing sophisticated facilitation, and responding to unexpected problems. Tired facilitators will also stop doing the "optional" (but important) tasks like walking the room and scanning for problems during exercises.

Breaks should theoretically help you as much as they help your audience. But as a friend once told me after teaching his first full-day workshop: "As soon as a break began, the attendees would immediately queue up to talk to me, and they just had so many questions. I didn't even get to eat."

Before and after the event, you're expected to be sociable. But the coffee and lunch breaks are yours and should be defended. Defending your breaks usually means hiding somewhere private; if the students can see you, they will find you. If the venue doesn't have a good hideaway room, just head outside.

You'll almost never get your entire break to yourself, but you should always get *some* of it. For example, you might need to spend the first five minutes helping a student whose questions you sidelined earlier. And you'll probably need to spend the final five minutes getting everyone back into their seats. But that still leaves a precious five minutes for you to put up your feet, close your eyes, take a few breaths, and ensure that you're at your best when the teaching resumes.

Lunch deserves special mention. If the food is obstructed by a queue, the students will surround you and bombard you with questions, turning your break into quite the opposite. As such, I typically try to get hold of a plate of food and then flee, like a seagull with a french-fry. I also keep a packed lunch in my workshop bag for situations where the catering looks like an inescapable trap.

Clients sometimes want to talk about business-y things at lunch. This is tricky since you'll usually want to be there for the networking and client relationship. Fortunately, a 60-minute lunch provides ample time for both eating and resting if you set good boundaries ahead of time:

> *"I'd love to join for lunch. But I'm going to need to leave 20 minutes early to give myself time to prepare for the next section. Will that be alright with everyone?"*

And remember, taking time for yourself isn't greedy. Your students deserve you at your best.

Lessons learned:

- Protecting your own energy is neither weak nor self-indulgent, but is required to continue doing a good job
- Ensure you have at least a few minutes of each break to yourself by hiding out of sight, even if that means leaving the building

Using co-teachers, expert guests, and helpers

An extra person on your teaching team can sometimes be the difference between a flop and a triumph. You've got four main options of who to bring (and some individuals will be able to fill multiple roles, of course):

- **Full co-teachers** with similar levels of teaching (and topic) expertise to yourself who are in charge of running a significant portion of the workshop
- **Expert guests** who can answer questions, tell stories, and deliver focused lecture segments, but who doesn't necessarily have any teaching or facilitation expertise
- **Facilitation helpers** who walk the room during exercises to help explain instructions and allow you to deal with larger crowds
- **Operational helpers** who can run off to deal with all the random things that can go wrong during a workshop (like missing coffee or a broken projector)

Co-teachers

Full co-teachers are obviously the most flexible (they can do everything), but they also tend to be expensive. Their role is self-explanatory. One facilitation caveat is to be careful not to undermine each other with too many interruptions, corrections, and addendums to what the other has said. Instead, decide who is leading each section, and then let them do so uninterrupted, even if you feel you have something clever or important to contribute. If the lead teacher wants help, they can explicitly ask the non-lead teacher to contribute.

A hidden benefit of a co-teacher is that they help you get better, faster. They can take notes on your performance (and you on theirs), and then you can swap notes and discuss what worked, what didn't, and what to try doing differently for next time. And if you're able to help at *their* gigs also, then you'll benefit from simply having more chances to practice, as well as more exposure to rare problems and unlikely edge cases. (And if you've got more time than money, swapping help like this is a viable alternative to paying each other.)

Expert guests

Expert guests are mainly used to lend extra credibility in an area where you feel a little weak. And since they'll usually enjoy dropping in for a guest lecture and to answer a few questions, they're often happy to do so for free.

While they're always a nice bonus, these types of guests can be an absolute godsend if you find yourself suffering from imposter syndrome. The worst imposter syndrome I ever felt was about seven years ago, when one of my self-organized workshops first passed

£10,000 in ticket sales. I was going crazy, imagining that everyone was going to storm out once they showed up and saw me. At the suggestion of my wonderful co-organizer, Adele, we invited four expert guests (one for each morning and afternoon of the two-day workshop) to give a short lecture and do a bit of Q&A—about 30 minutes total. As a nice bonus, they each ended up staying through the break after their segment, giving the students a chance to chat and mingle. The guests added a level of credibility which I never could have achieved on my own, and all it "cost" was a little bit of organizing.

The downside of expert guests is that you can't really guarantee the quality or relevance of what they're going to say. Having learned this particular lesson the hard way, I now avoid asking guests to deliver core Learning Outcomes. Instead, I have them *complement* the Learning Outcomes by adding a fresh and credible perspective, a personal story, or some additional examples and exercises. The guests then become massively beneficial while also being less of a liability. So if they end up delivering a standup comedy routine instead of an educational lecture, the workshop can still achieve its goal.

You also need to know what to do when they go fully off the reservation. I once had an expert guest show up very late and very drunk, and then proceed to yell at my audience about how they would never be successful like him. This was unfortunate because he actually *had* been successful in the notoriously difficult niche of independent journalism, which the audience was razor-keen to learn about. I didn't know how to handle it at the time, so I just gritted my teeth while allowing him to destroy my event. But I've since learned the correct solution, and it doesn't even require any confrontation.

If a guest is going wildly off-track, you're going to need to interrupt them in the middle of whatever they're saying by grabbing two chairs and carrying them onto the stage with a flourish and a big grin. You're going to put down the chairs, sit down in one while gesturing toward the other, and say:

> *"Hope you don't mind me jumping in here. You were saying some super interesting stuff earlier that I wanted to dig into a bit more. Would you mind if we switch into a bit of an interview so I can explore some of it with you?"*

Or:

> *"I hope you'll forgive my interruption, but there's some fascinating stuff in your history that I know everyone here would love to hear more about. Would you mind if I jump in here with some questions so I can get your take on a few of the big moments in your life and career?"*

And then run the rest of their session as a moderated conversation, optionally shifting into an open Q&A once you're ready. Most speakers in this situation will be glad for your intervention; they're aware they've been rambling and are feeling uncomfortable, but don't know how to fix it. By jumping in, you're handing them a non-awkward lifeline. And if a guest *does* perceive it as a slap on the wrist, they'll at least appreciate that you did so in a way which kept up appearances.

Facilitation helpers

Facilitation helpers are volunteers who you've lightly trained ahead of time to help attendees understand and complete complex exercises. You explain the situation in detail to your helper and then, during the exercise itself, they can run around the room with to help unstick attendees. If I know I'll need someone for this, I typically just grab an over-eager student or venue employee before starting and ask them to help me out for the section in question. But if it's critical (and/or you require several helpers), then you'll likely need to organize and train them in advance.

I used to regularly co-teach a fun workshop on business model innovation. It worked brilliantly but required enough 1-on-1 help that it could only handle audiences of up to about 30. So when my team was asked to teach it in Bulgaria to an audience of 300, we recruited ten volunteers from the local startup community, spent half an hour training them, and then put each of them in charge of a tenth of the audience while we kept an eye on the bigger picture.

In an ideal world, your exercise prompts would be perfectly clear and your workshop would be scalable enough to handle arbitrarily large audiences. But since that's almost never fully attainable, a facilitation helper is a great way to fill in the gaps.

Operational helpers

Operational helpers spend most of their time just sitting idle, and then occasionally leap into action to deal with anything that goes wrong with the venue, catering, operations, logistics, equipment, or anything else. They don't require any special skills beyond being good with people and willing to solve unexpected problems. Small and simple events don't require a helper and bigger events will often include a helper provided by the venue or client. But in cases where you can't count on that, hiring a good helper (on a freelance, hourly basis) can be very worthwhile.

My best-ever helper was Lucy, who I poached from her job as a bar manager after seeing her perform repeatedly (and brilliantly) as a host and problem-solver.[18] The number of times she saved my bacon are too numerous to list, but I'll share the most memorable. I had been informed, the evening before a full-day event, that my venue had somehow become unavailable. I spent a minute or two cursing cruel fate and then started looking for solutions. After calling half a dozen venues, I found a viable replacement. Great! But it was near London Bridge, a 20-minute drive from the original Shoreditch location. I couldn't expect attendees to receive an alert about the change of address before morning, and I didn't want to abandon anyone who happened to miss it. I called Lucy to strategize and we agreed on a plan.

The next morning, I arrived early at the original, cancelled venue to find her already waiting, along with a half dozen taxis and a pile of cheap umbrellas (it was a drizzly London morning). Once enough folks had arrived, I traveled with the first car to get the new venue set up while she stood guard at the original venue to shuttle over any late arrivals. We ended up having a great day and every single person made it over to the

---

[18] I think lots of folks in service jobs share this quality, and that they're widely under-utilized as a talent pool to hire from. They're easy to find, and you can accurately judge their skills by simply becoming a regular. They can also get started on part-time projects without quitting their day job. Lucy is now a university teacher.

new location (eventually including Lucy, who arrived about two hours later along with the final participant).

Operational hiccups are rarely this dramatic, but they're always important. Even if it isn't a showstopper, something like missing coffee or a faulty projector can be a real thorn in your side and is extremely difficult to solve on your own without creating a big interruption in the event.

Lessons learned:

- Co-teachers help deliver the core material and allow you to improve faster
- Expert guests provide a credibility boost, and can be included (via lecture, interviews, Q&A) as a complement to your core teaching material
- Facilitation helpers support larger audiences by walking the room and unsticking confused attendees during key exercises
- Operational helpers can deal with anything else which comes up during the day

What to do when everything goes wrong

Sometimes, stuff will go wrong which is *really not your fault*. The projector will break, the venue will catch fire, and someone will bring along a baby who throws up all over you and your computer. That's fine. It's not a big deal.

The show must go on

The golden rule of workshop disasters is this: **the audience mirrors your panic. If you're cool with it, they're cool with it.** Shrug it off, adjust the plan, and keep on keeping on.

I recently ran a session in Copenhagen where a fire alarm forced us to evacuate. It was unscheduled, so we needed to wait for the fire department to show up. Once we got outside, I faced a decision. On the one hand, I could take the easy option of claiming it wasn't my fault (which was true) and that there was nothing I could do (which wasn't). Or, alternately, I could create a path forward.

I glanced around to locate the event organizer, walked over, and told him that—assuming he was okay with it—I would like to gather everyone around and continue teaching outside. There was a nearby wall I could stand on, surrounded by plenty of flat, empty space for the audience. I normally would have moved them over there myself, but the organizer took the initiative and did a great job of announcing the new plan with a wink and a smile:

> *"Hello everyone, welcome to Copenhagen's wonderful outdoors. We will continue the event from that wall over there, so if you'd like to follow me and find a spot, we will get going again. A lovely and pleasant surprise, wouldn't you say?"*

Meanwhile, I climbed up on the wall and started talking in circles. Everyone soon wandered over and we ended up having a great event.

Inexperienced facilitators tend to dread this sort of situation, expecting an audience to resist—or even rebel against—the sudden change in plan. But the attendees are aware that the whims of the universe are not within your control. So although it's true that they don't especially want to hear excuses or apologies, they will *gladly* support you in any plausible plan to continue moving forward, no matter how strange or unlikely. That's why everyone was willing to accept a cab ride after my unexpected venue switch. And it's why everyone in Copenhagen walked happily over to the wall.

If something happens which is impossible to roll with, then keep calm and call a coffee break:

> *"Hey folks, this is obviously a bit unexpected and I'm going to need a couple minutes to sort it out so we can continue with the learning. The good news is, that means you get a bonus coffee break. Hold tight, grab some refreshments, and I'll update you as soon as possible."*[19]

You now have 5-15 minutes to find a path forward. And remember, that does *not* mean you need to find a way to do exactly what you originally intended. Depending on what went wrong, "Plan A" might be well and truly over. If the projector is broken, then the projector is broken, and you're going to need to find a way to succeed without it. But remember, folks didn't show up for Plan A... they showed up to receive a set of Learning Outcomes. Your workshop is a success so long as you can succeed in that one task, no matter how different it ends up looking from the original plan.

In the case of equipment failure, you can usually ask to borrow anything that your students have brought with them, which includes anything hidden

---

[19] This is one of the (many) reasons that refreshments should be available all day instead of being brought out just for breaks.

away in their bags. As ridiculous as it sounds, I've had to borrow a computer from the audience no fewer than five times. Once due to the theft of my power cable while walking to the venue, once when an excited attendee dropped a pint of cider onto my laptop, and once when a super high-resolution projector somehow overwhelmed my computer's humble brain. The others were just normal, mundane tech problems. Although most of these were at fairly casual events, two were during well-paid, high-profile corporate gigs. I made it into a little joke, everyone had a laugh, and somebody in the front row handed me a fresh computer. I grabbed the backup of my slides from the cloud (you do have a backup of your slides in the cloud, right?) and kept on teaching. Easy breezy.[20]

Reduce your exposure to bad luck

It's also worth noting that you can control your own exposure to bad luck, taking steps—in advance—to prevent many types of bad luck from ever being able to strike.

The first 80% of reliability is trivial, and you can start doing it right now, simply by choosing to make the effort. It includes stuff like

---

[20] I'm not sure there's an exact prescription for fostering this sort of mental state, but I believe it involves a) being well-rested, b) understanding that your audience wants you to succeed rather than fail, and c) setting aside your sense of self (and self-judgement) for the duration of the workshop. If a wolf gets into a shepherd's herd, the shepherd doesn't take time to indulge in a pity party. Instead, he deals with the wolf problem, and then finishes getting his sheep to wherever they're going, and then has a beer, and *then* takes time to reflect on what went wrong. It's the same thing with your students.

- Basic logistics, like flying to an event one day early so you have time to book another flight if yours gets delayed or cancelled, and showing up to the venue early enough to look at your room
- Simple professionalism, like good client communication and having your workshop designed and refined in advance
- Mundane preparedness, like bringing your own adaptors/plugs/cables and having a backup of your slides on a USB key and online

We've already covered these basics, but I'm repeating them here as a reminder, and to encourage you to actually do them. Folks tend not to take the basics seriously enough, and you're leaving money on the table if you don't.

The rest of your exposure to bad luck comes from the complexity of the workshop design itself and the number of external dependencies like supplies or equipment. As a general rule, you can reduce your workshop's fragility (i.e. its vulnerability to bad luck) in four ways:

1. If you can simplify your facilitation/storytelling requirements without compromising the quality of the education, then simplify it
2. If you depend on something which you can carry, then bring it yourself instead of expecting the venue to provide it
3. If you can't bring it yourself, then you must be extremely proactive about ensuring that the venue/client has gotten it there
4. If you can't guarantee you'll get what you need, then be prepared to delete the vulnerable section and replace it with something else

Do you rely on wifi and a sound system? Then bring your own mobile hotspot and bluetooth speaker system. Nobody cares as much about your workshop as you do, so don't trust the venue (or whoever else) to solve your problems. Or if you rely on playing a YouTube video, then find a way to download it ahead of time and bring it with you.

Supplies like printouts, paper, pens, and sticky notes deserve special mention. Venues always claim to be able to provide these basics, and they are (almost) always lying. If it's too much for you to carry, then ship it ahead of time in a big box, early enough that you can send another one if the first gets lost or held in customs.

A lot of "bad luck" can be prevented by being more proactive in your client/venue communications. I was once asked to teach a session in Romania about creative entrepreneurship and designed it with frequent switching and rearranging of groups to keep the energy high and the discussions fresh. I had told the client that I would need cabaret seating, or at least rearrangeable seating, and they had promised that I would have it. But since the seating really mattered, I sent them an email a few days before the event to verify, asking for some photos of the actual room I would be in. And then, when they didn't send the photos, I called them on the phone and asked (nicely) if they could turn on video and walk through the venue right then to show me how it looked.

As it happened, my requirements had gotten lost in the shuffle, and they had put me in a very beautiful—and equally non-viable—theatre with fixed-row seating. Thanks to my proactive check-in, they were able to switch my room with a smaller, but more flexible one, and my session went smoothly. (If they hadn't been able to switch my room, I would have had to redesign my whole workshop to fit the new room constraints.

That would have been annoying, but still far better than being blindsided once I got there.)

It's theoretically the venue or client's job to remember and adhere to your requirements, and to update you if anything changes. But they've got a million priorities which are higher on the list than your workshop. If you depend on something which is being provided by someone else, then it's worth going above and beyond to guarantee that it's there.

Run a retrospective after every workshop

In UK schools, teachers are tasked with self-improvement through "reflective practice". The idea is to sit down with a notebook after each day's teaching and list out everything that went wrong, everything that went unusually well, why those things might have happened, and what you might try doing differently to get less of the former and more of the latter. The idea is to turn yourself into a learning machine, gobbling up your classroom experiences and transmuting them into your own personal lessons learned.

I agree and have been doing retros after every workshop since the very beginning. It usually only takes 10 or 20 minutes. If you have a co-teacher (or trusted spectator), then do it with them. Otherwise, do it yourself. The end result should be a small number of clearly defined, high-impact changes that you'll make for next time. You won't be able to solve every problem (or replicate every win) every time, but you should always attempt a couple of them.

A feedback form isn't required to figure out what went wrong. Feedback forms certainly have their place and are crucial for proving to clients that you did a good job, and also for collecting attendee testimonials.

But most workshop problems are fairly self-evident (sloppy operations, low energy, bad venue, confusing exercises, ineffective lecture, slipped schedule, slow crowd control, confused attendees, hostile or distracting individual, etc.). Once you start looking for—and taking note of—these issues, you'll be able to find most of what matters with a quick retrospective.

This isn't about beating yourself up, but rather about finding ways to improve. Over time, these improvements compound, and one day you'll finish a session and think to yourself, "Wow, that actually went pretty damn well."

Lessons learned:

- The audience mirrors your panic; if you're cool with it, they're cool with it
- Bad luck can be reduced by bringing your own supplies and through extremely proactive client/venue communication
- After each workshop, run a short retrospective

Serve the people in the room, even if there aren't so many of them

What if you design a great workshop, but only a couple people buy tickets or show up? What should you do? Perhaps you can already guess at my advice: you should proceed. No matter how many of them there are, the people in the room are the right people. If there are fewer than you had hoped, then you can carve out some time in the future—the next day, perhaps—to reflect on why, and to rethink your marketing and messaging. But for the time being, right now, while you're facing a sea of empty seats, you are going to clear your mind of all such thoughts, and you will proceed.

If folks are spread out, as they are likely to be, then ask everyone to grab a new seat, closer to you, at the front. You might choose to push aside most of the chairs, arranging the few required into a small circle or around a single table. Instead of trying to shout into a big space which will always feel empty, create a small space which seems full. Resist the urge to repeatedly delay your starting time in the vain hope that dozens more people will suddenly appear. Focus on those who are there, not those who aren't. Remind your attendees—and yourself, if needed—that this is *great news*, because you'll really be able to get into it together.

Treat the small group as a rare opportunity to gather deep insight into what your audience cares about, which will pay dividends for all future workshops. You can hear about their hopes (of what they want to learn and achieve), their fears (of why they haven't already), and their frustrations (about where they've gotten stuck before). These small sessions are a goldmine of learning, and you can really set the standard of how well you intend to educate the people who have put their faith in you.

Lessons learned:

- Instead of worrying about under-attended workshops, just gather everyone toward the front and do a great job for them

Summary of Part 2 (and a facilitation checklist):

The week before:

- Confirm audience profile and numbers with event organizer
- Confirm the room setup with the organizer or venue
- Confirm that stationary, supplies, and printouts are ordered and accounted for

Your workshop bag:

- Clicker (and batteries)
- Backup slides (on a USB stick and in the cloud)
- Projector adaptors (for both VGA and HDMI)
- Power adaptors
- Classroom timer and exercise timer
- Fresh whiteboard markers (just in case)
- Bluetooth speaker (if using videos or music)
- Stationary and supplies (if you're the one bringing it)

The Workshop Survival Guide

The morning of:

- Put a physical copy of your Workshop Skeleton in your pocket (including Learning Outcomes, section timings, and key exercises)

Upon arrival:

- Visually confirm the room setup (and make any emergency improvements)
- Test the projector, clicker, wifi, power, and any other required equipment
- Close any extraneous computer programs (especially those with unpredictable notifications like chat, email, and file-synching)
- Mute your phone and, if using it as an exercise timer, change the settings so you won't have to keep unlocking it to check the time
- Confirm that coffee and/or food will be available when expected

During your workshop:

- If you're going to start late, tell people
- Intros should be short; the value is in your content, not you
- Stop standing behind the podium (use a clicker and stand at the front of the stage)
- Stop glancing at your phone (use a watch or classroom timer)
- Finish group formation before assigning a task; manually fix uneven groups and stranded individuals
- During an exercise, walk the room to listen in on students working
- When asking a student to share, have them stand and speak toward the crowd

- You can control a crowd by going individual
- To silence a distracted crowd, just start talking (in circles) or ask a student volunteer to share (borrowing goodwill)
- Nobody in the audience *wants* to be hostile or disengaged, so there's usually a good reason which you can discover (and resolve) if you search for it
- Protect your breaks by hiding out of sight
- Finishing on time is extremely valuable, and often worth cutting content to achieve
- Most "bad luck" can be solved via either better preparation or by bringing along a co-teacher, expert guest, or helper
- When bad luck strikes anyway, shrug it off and find a way to continue teaching

Conclusion and final thoughts

Rob here. I used to be a terrible (and terrified) public speaker. After my first international talk, I was so desperate to flee that I accidentally rushed out through the fire escape. In an early guest lecture at a university, I misjudged the distance to the whiteboard (it stood out from the wall by half a meter) and ran into it when I turned around, knocking myself flat on my back in front of 500 grad students (who somehow all seemed to have their phones out and filming). When I needed to start making video tutorials for one of my businesses, I was too nervous to show my face, so I recorded them as voiceovers of my screen. And even that would keep me up at night.

What I'm trying to say is that this stuff didn't come naturally to me.

But then, several years later, I was back at that same university (the one where I fell over), giving a short session about some of my startup experiences. Afterwards, a guy named John walked up and said:

"Wow, you got good at this. I mean, it was so much better. You used to be terrible!"

I said thanks (sort of), and he ended up hiring me for my first set of paid teaching gigs at the unbelievable rate (or so I thought at the time) of £800 per day. This was a super exciting milestone, since it proved to me that I was actually improving. Since then, I've seen my rates creep slowly upward to the point where I was earning more in an afternoon than I used to in a month.

I never figured out any big "trick" or "secret" to getting better rates. Rather, I found that my pay stayed more or less in lockstep with my skills. As I put in the work and figured out how to succeed more deeply and more reliably with my students, my pay increased to match. The other stuff—sales, proposals, client communications, etc.—is obviously something you'll need to be able to deal with, but it isn't what you get paid for. So the "trick", insofar as one exists, is to get really good at the craft of teaching.

With this in mind, I humbly suggest you take the long view on developing your skills.

You don't learn to play guitar by trying *really hard* for one week. You learn it by loving the craft (and occasionally hating it) and continuing to practice regardless for several years. And then, one day, you find yourself capturing the full attention of a crowd with your music. And people in the audience are like, "Man, I wish I could do that." Mastering a craft is about staying in the game. Keep trying, forgive yourself your mistakes, and get better every day.

One of the reasons I find education so fascinating is that there's always a fresh challenge to solve. Some of the students aren't learning… But why? And what can I change to fix it? Can I adjust the energy levels?

The Learning Outcomes? The social dynamics within the groups? The facilitation? Can I use a different metaphor, a different Teaching Format, or a clearer exercise prompt? Can I invent something else entirely? I've been trying to learn how to teach for some time now, and there's still so much more to do. I love it, and I hope you will too. Even in the cases where there's no clear right answer, and it's hard, and it's scary, and all we can do is our best.

Thanks for reading. Hope it was helpful. If you have any comments or questions, you can reach us at:

- Rob Fitzpatrick: rob@robfitz.com
- Devin Hunt: devin@hailpixel.com
- More resources: http://workshopsurvival.com

If you feel inclined to help *us* out, the best way to do so is by posting an Amazon review, sending us feedback and suggestions, or recommending this book to a friend or colleague.

We wish the very best to both you and your students.

Appendix: Advanced Teaching Formats

The Appendix contains a collection of advanced Teaching Formats, plus an example of testing and refining a new exercise design.

These new Formats aren't exactly "better" but are certainly more *specific*. They'll help you succeed at unusual educational challenges and to teach difficult Learning Outcomes which are normally hard to make stick.

I'd suggest skimming through the overview below, and then skipping to the Formats which seem most relevant to your particular topics and interests.

Here's a summary of the advanced Formats:

Specialty Teaching Formats	
Trigger Questions (rapid-fire scenarios and idea generation)	Helps generate ideas and reveal alternative solutions via a series of quick prompts to keep redoing the same situation in different ways
Card Games	For introducing lots of tools, options, or resources using a variety of playful and engaging games and activities
Putting on the judging hat	For teaching skills where success is determined by an external third party whose judgement is neither "fair" nor transparent (e.g. applying for a job or raising funding)
Lab time	For letting attendees spend large blocks of time working on their own projects, with expert help available if they run into problems

Plenty of fun options. Let's get into how to use them.

Format: Trigger Questions for escaping tunnel-vision

Trigger Questions are a series of prompts to force the attendees to **repeatedly solve the same problem in different ways**, usually under very tight time restrictions (i.e. 2-5 minutes per prompt). The quick timing leads to fun, frantic energy and is often a high point for the workshop. Alternately, you can allow more time per prompt and run a slower, more thoughtful exercise.

Apart from the fun, what's the benefit of this Format? The main issue is that learners tend to get tunnel-vision, fixating on the *first* solution they can think of, and then refining it to the exclusion of seeing other options. As such, if you give people an hour to work on something, most will spend the whole time "perfecting" their *first* idea, even if that idea is fundamentally flawed. But by using Trigger Questions to force them to restart several times, and to use a different—and potentially unnatural—approach each time, you can carry them safely past this trap. And as a happy side effect, they'll often end up with a pile of ideas.

In his wonderful book, *Anything You Want*, Derek Sivers shares the following story of learning to sing from a great coach named Warren Senders:

> *For each lesson, I'd bring in one song I was trying to improve.*
>
> *First, I'd sing it for him as written.*
>
> *Then he'd say, "OK—now do it up an octave."*
>
> *"Uh... up an octave? But I can't sing that high!"*
>
> *"I don't care! Do it anyway! Go! 1... 2... 3... 4..."*
>
> *I'd sing the whole song again, in screeching squeaking falsetto, sounding like a choking mouse. But by the second half of the song, it was almost charming.*
>
> *Then he'd say, "OK—now do it down an octave."*

"Down an octave? But I don't think I can!"

"Doesn't matter! Go! 1... 2... 3... 4..."

I sounded like a garbage disposal or lawn mower, but he made me sing the whole song that way.

Then he'd make me sing it twice as fast. Then twice as slow. Then like Bob Dylan. Then like Tom Waits. Then he'd tell me to sing it like it's 4 a.m. and a friend woke me up. Then he'd give me many other scenarios.

After all of this, he'd say, "Now... how did that song go again?"

What an amazing way to break someone out of a mental rut! And while Derek's example is obviously from a 1-on-1 scenario, you can easily adapt it to work with larger audiences by just planning your triggers ahead of time and putting each of them on a slide.

For example, if you were helping youths figure out how to introduce themselves for their upcoming job interview (or public talk), you might run them through a series of Trigger Questions like this:

*Okay, we're going to try out a bunch of different ways of introducing ourselves. First, you're going to give your introduction **like you normally would, if you were meeting a new friend.** I want you to take 2 minutes to write down the most important points you'd like to share, and then you'll each have 1 minute to introduce yourself to your group. Okay, start writing.*

*Alright, now you've got 2 minutes to write a new intro, but this time I want you write it **as if it was your supportive granny giving the intro**, who thinks you're* *just the greatest. This might feel a little strange to talk about how great you are like she would, but just give it a try. Two minutes to write, and then afterwards you'll each have 1 minute to share. Ready? Go!*

Okay, now do it totally neutrally, like it was a newspaper reporter describing the facts about your life in as few words as possible. Same as before, 2 minutes to write, 1 minute to share.

Okay, now this time...

You can generalize this approach to any number of topics. If you were teaching pottery, you could have them throw a bowl as if they were already famous and could get away with being impossibly minimalistic. And then as if they lived in the developing world and were simply making something for their family to eat from. And then as if they were exploring new shapes and planning to discard the experiment as soon as it was done.

If you were working with aspiring restaurateurs, you could ask them to redesign their dream restaurant if they only had 10m^2 (100ft^2) of floor space, and then with only two employees (one chef, one server), and then as a catering service for weddings and events, and then as a takeaway joint, and then in a location with no on-site kitchen, or in partnership with a nearby farm. Having spent a couple minutes apiece on these silly little "make-believe" exercises, they're now starting to think:

Wait a minute... If I go for something much smaller than I was originally thinking, and have a more limited menu, then I might be able to skip paying for a proper kitchen and instead just get licensed to prepare the food off-site. That would mean I wouldn't even need the bank loan, so I could get started immediately!

This is how folks escape from tunnel-vision and start seeing fresh approaches. Telling someone to pause their dreams to "start small and grow from there" is a platitude which they will ignore 100% of the time. Even if it's the correct approach, imploring them to follow your hard-won advice is an example of *telling* vs. *teaching*. Instead, allow them to experience that revelation for themselves—before losing their money—by having them work through a wide variety of rapid-fire scenarios.

By using the Trigger Questions to constrain folks into narrow (but fruitful) areas of thought, they'll end up with a larger number of more interesting ideas than they would have been able to invent on their own. They also get to walk away with a big list of their own ideas, which everyone loves.

Trigger Questions are fast, fun, and can be super high energy. They're great for either idea generation or for rapid-fire scenarios to build skills and escape tunnel-vision. Of course, if you want it to run smoothly, you'll need to pay extra attention to having good prompts and crowd control. But the payoff is huge.

Lessons learned:

- Trigger Questions are a series of quick, rapid-fire prompts to get folks attacking the same problem multiple times, in multiple ways
- Use Trigger Questions to help students escape tunnel-vision and generate ideas

Format: Putting on the judging hat

Imagine you're running a workshop to help disadvantaged youths prepare for their upcoming job interviews. The Learning Outcomes for this topic include a whole cluster of wisdom/skill hybrids: how to introduce yourself while walking the line between bravado and timidity, what to highlight (and what to skip) on your CV, how to answer tough questions that you really don't have an answer to, and plenty more.

As a teacher trying to convey this sort of material, you've got three big challenges. The first is that you can't possibly prepare them for every permutation and obstacle, so you need to give them a functional mental model for the thoughts of the recruiter or interviewer (i.e. the "judge"). The second is that some of the stuff which matters—like spending the time to write a bespoke cover letter and proofread it—won't *seem* important, so it falls victim to the teaching-vs-telling trap and then gets ignored. And lastly, even if an attendee learns all the skills and does everything perfectly, there's still a high chance that they don't get the job for reasons completely beyond their own control.

Lots of topics carry this "external judge" dynamic: fundraising, dating, getting a job, applying to university, getting a publisher/label/agent, finding freelance work, getting a bank loan, and countless others.

I struggled for *years* to crack this challenge before finally stumbling across the solution of "putting on the judging hat". It's based around a simple idea: before teaching people how to do something that will be judged by someone else, first have them spend some time acting as the judge.

If you're teaching folks to write a killer CV, first have them act as recruiters, where they'll review 12 CVs and decide which three to interview. Have them do it in groups, and to discuss and document their reasons for eliminating (or shortlisting) certain candidates. Ensure that there are too many good candidates, so some will be eliminated on a coin flip. Others will be *almost* perfect, but with some sloppy typos or bad design. Allow these young people to *experience* how, as an employer (or any sort of judge), a seemingly harmless mistake can act as an easy reason to eliminate an otherwise promising applicant.

Before I teach fundraising, I like to start with a simple, 3-minute (plus discussion) Judging Hat exercise to get the attendees to better understand the investor's perspective. Here's the prompt:

> *Imagine you're an investor interested in high-risk, high-returns tech businesses. I'm going to show you four businesses. In your groups, you're going to rank them*

Business A			Business B		
Brilliant Team	Patented IP	Widely covered in the press	£10k Monthly revenue	Happy customers	Very slow growth

Business C		Business D		
£350k Raised via kickstarter	New urban clothing brand	20k Weekly active users	7% Week-on-week growth	£0.00 No revenue

> *from most investable to least investable.*

Now, here's the thing: all four of these businesses are doing great, in their own way, and all of them are worth continuing to work on. But only one of them is "good" in the *particular way* that appeals to most tech investors. Which means that although the other three can still grow into great businesses, they're unlikely to be able to raise early-stage funding. This is a powerful insight for aspiring entrepreneurs, because it shows that a business can be a *good* without being *investable*. And conversely, that an investor's disinterest does not necessarily mean that a business is doomed. And also, that if they *want* early-stage investment, then they need to select their idea and build their business in a certain way. These are subtle, sophisticated takeaways that I've *only* been able to teach with the help of the Judging Hat.

In terms of energy levels, putting on the judging hat is fun. People enjoy both the exercise itself and also its insight about how the world works. It can be facilitated under tight time constraints with high energy, or it can be done as a slower, more thoughtful exercise.

Remember the three goals of this format:

1. Give students a reasonable mental model of the "judge", so they can start to reason about what matters and what's correct, even if they haven't been drilled on every permutation
2. Allow them to experience, from the judge's perspective, why certain tiny mistakes and best practices can have a disproportionately large impact on your results
3. Show them that sometimes, even perfect applicants get rejected, and that doesn't necessarily mean the applicant failed or is in any way unworthy

The Judging Hat succeeds brilliantly at all three goals. Facilitation is identical to running any other

Scenario Challenge. The important difference is the shift in perspective (from "doer" to "judge") during the task.

Lessons learned:

- Certain topics exist where "success" is dependent on the judgement of some external, opaque, and sometimes arbitrary evaluator (i.e. college applications, jobs, dating, and many creative fields)
- Simply teaching these skills isn't enough—you also need to have folks "Put on the Judging Hat" so they can wrap their head around the evaluation and decision-making process they'll be subjected to

Format: Card games

Card games are brilliantly high-energy and are surprisingly applicable in educational workshops. Creating the materials requires a bit of preparation, but the upside is worth it.

Cards are uniquely good at introducing and explaining a long list of tools, options, or resources. They're also a fun, fast way to facilitate Scenario Challenges. Throughout this section, we'll look at a variety of games and activities, each with its own educational specialty.

One of the business books I love to teach is *Traction*, by Weinberg and Mares. Beyond offering a helpful theoretical framework for how to grow a business, it also provides a clear set of 20 options for how successful businesses managed to start getting noticed. Of course,

20 options would be a lot to talk through, requiring the better part of an hour and liable to become punishingly dull. This is a perfect situation for cards.

The design for these cards can be simple. All it needs is a name for each option, plus a short description of what it's all about:

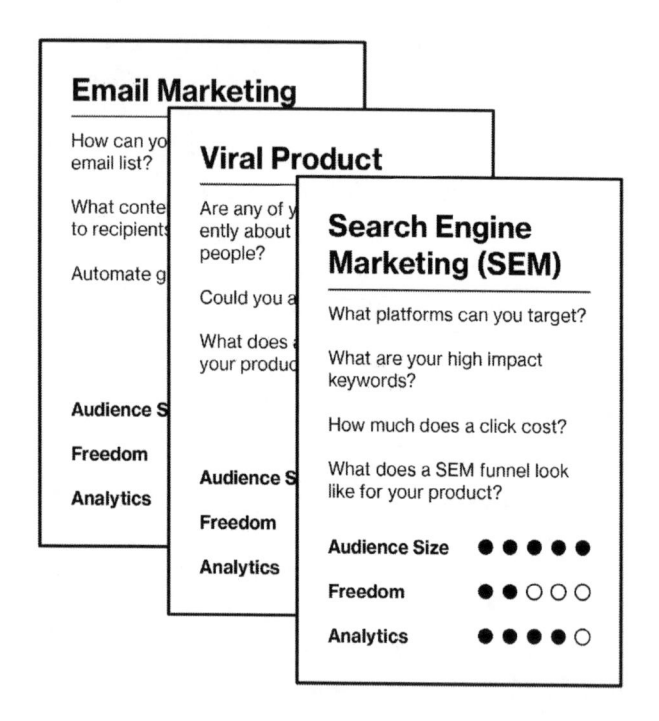

Email Marketing

How can yo[u] email list?

What conte[nt] to recipients

Automate g[...]

Audience S[ize]

Freedom

Analytics

Viral Product

Are any of y[...] ently about [...] people?

Could you a[...]

What does [...] your produ[ct]

Audience S[ize]

Freedom

Analytics

Search Engine Marketing (SEM)

What platforms can you target?

What are your high impact keywords?

How much does a click cost?

What does a SEM funnel look like for your product?

Audience Size ● ● ● ● ●

Freedom ● ● ○ ○ ○

Analytics ● ● ● ● ○

By putting each of the 20 options on its own card, you can then facilitate a number of fun and frantic exercises while simultaneously introducing the class to all the options. For example:

> "Shuffle the cards and deal out 3 to each person. Now, you've got 2 minutes. **Pick your favorite** from the 3 you've been given and come up with an idea (or a way to use that option) based on what it tells you."

*"Spread the cards on the table. **Pick the craziest or most difficult** one you can find, and hand it to the person to your right. Work on whatever you've been given. You've got three minutes to come up with as many plausible ways to use it as you can."*

*"Leave the cards in the center, face down. Pick one up at random, come up with an idea as quickly as possible, and then put it back and pick up another card. Try to **get through as many of the cards as possible**. If you find a card you really hate, just come up with a dumb idea for it and then move on. You've got five minutes. Try to get through all 20. Go!"*

The above isn't exactly a "game", but rather a playful variant of either Scenario Challenges or Trigger Questions. You can repeat these sorts of prompts (with a bit of variation) near endlessly to expose attendees to as many of the options as you like, in a fun and engaging fashion.

Of course, there are loads of playful uses for cards, and some of them certainly become more game-like. Here are a couple options:

Best at X: This game works like *Top Trumps*. In addition to the name and description, each card is ranked on a scale of 1-5 on several criteria. For example, cards of marketing tools might include ratings for "audience size", "analytics", and "creative freedom".

Sitting in groups of 3-5, each player has a hand of

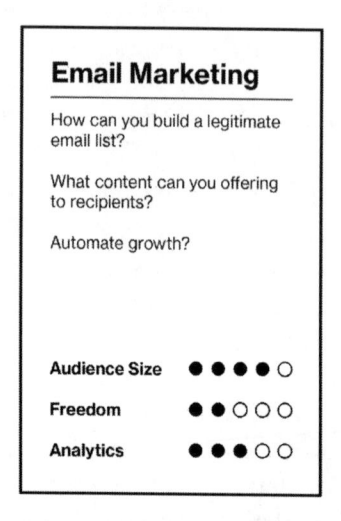

> **Email Marketing**
>
> How can you build a legitimate email list?
>
> What content can you offering to recipients?
>
> Automate growth?
>
> Audience Size ● ● ● ● ○
> Freedom ● ● ○ ○ ○
> Analytics ● ● ● ○ ○

three cards. The winner of the previous hand plays a card, while also choosing one of its criteria to compete on, and simultaneously explaining to the rest of their group why their card is great for that particular purpose:

> "I play the card 'Facebook Ads' to compete on 'Audience Size' with a score of 5/5 because it has a bazillion users and includes all types of people."

Everyone else then plays a card to "compete" on the same criteria, and the player with the highest rating (in the chosen dimension) wins the hand. The winner collects the played cards, leaving them on the table in front of them as a "point". In the case of a draw, the tied players each make a short argument about why their option is superior for the chosen criteria, and then the group votes on who has won. All players draw a new card and play repeats until the deck and hands are empty.

The gameplay itself isn't terribly deep or interesting. But the arguments in favor of one card or another certainly can be. The main point is to ensure that everyone in each group has at least some passing exposure to the relative strengths and weaknesses of each option.

Card Sort: Like "best at X", Card Sorts also allow for comparisons between the options' strengths and similarities. It's one of the easiest to facilitate: each person takes a card from the deck, and then places it somewhere on the table. After they place one, they draw another and continue until the whole pile is sorted to their satisfaction. You can arrange the sorting in two ways: as either open clusters or on a 2x2 grid.

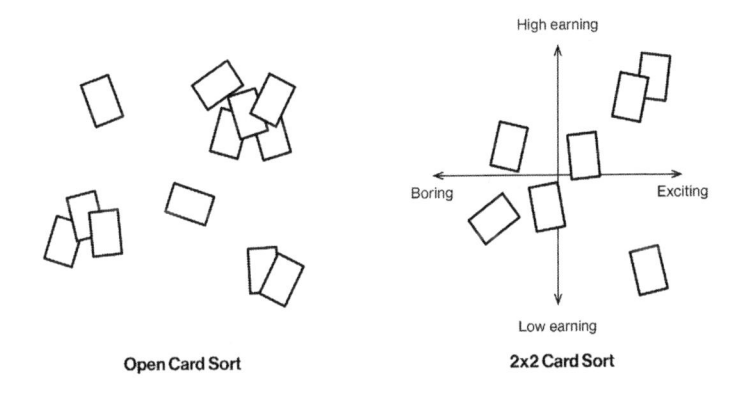

Open Card Sort

2x2 Card Sort

In an unstructured "open" Card Sort, you simply ask attendees to put similar cards near to each other in clusters, until they've found a place for the whole deck. This exercise can lead to powerful discussions about what the categories and comparisons should even be. For example, in a career planning workshop, you might ask high schoolers to Card Sort a number of job options.

And while the options listed on the cards might be useful, a bigger lesson is in the debate over whether to think of jobs as "part time vs. full-time" or "remote vs. local" or "boring vs. fun" or "profit vs. passion". The categories they create will be shifting and uncertain, but the debate leading up to those categories holds clear value for certain topics.

In a 2x2 Card Sort, you modify the above by telling the participants which metrics they should consider when ranking and placing each card. For example, you might ask them to sort careers on a 2x2 where one axis is "high-earning vs. low-earning" and another axis is "excites me vs. bores me". And then, a few minutes later, you could throw them for a loop by asking them to resort the same cards along a different set of criteria, which would cause new options to bubble to the top. (e.g. axes of "I'd learn a lot vs. I'd be stagnant" and "Growing industry vs. declining industry"). The choice of criteria will dictate the type of conversation they have, and can also provide a meta-lesson in how to evaluate options.

Answer the question / Fill in the blank: This game works like *Cards Against Humanity*. In addition to the resource cards, you also create a separate set of cards which each contain a short prompt, question, challenge, or fill-in-the-blank. For example, some "challenge cards" for a marketing exercise might include:

> "How can we most cost-effectively reach our market of rebellious teenagers? Why?"

> "As a small company targeting larger enterprises, we should begin by using _____."

"We're doing an exploratory campaign where analytics and insight matter more than actual sales. What do you suggest and why?"

"_____ is better than _____ because..."

"I would never use _____ because..."

Each player holds a hand of a few "answer cards", which are the same resources or options used in the previous exercises. The new deck of "challenge cards" are on the table, face-down, in a stack. The active player draws the next prompt card and reads it out.

Everyone else responds to the prompt by playing a card from their hand, while also giving a short explanation of why it works for this scenario. The active player (who has drawn and read the challenge card, but not played a solution) then picks their favorite answer, and the winning player takes the stack of used cards (placed on the table) to represent a point. Everyone refills their hand (assuming more resource cards still exist), and the next "active" player (going clockwise) draws the next prompt.

In the original game, *Cards Against Humanity*, the answers are provided anonymously (to avoid biased judgement) by placing them face-down on the table and shuffling them. But in the workshop version, the discussion is more important than the card itself, so anonymity is sacrificed in favor of allowing each player to explain the virtues of their solution.

Building a narrative: This game works like *Rory's Story Cubes*, but with less randomization. This is a slower, more thoughtful exercise where attendees combine multiple cards, in a certain order, to create a "narrative" about how they might solve a given scenario. For example, in a wedding planning workshop, you might have cards with different types of venues, activities and entertainments, plus any other ways to fill the time. Participants could then grab a selection of cards to quickly draft out the schedule of their own potential wedding, or to create an event in response to a specific challenge scenario.

Or if you were teaching a workshop about what you've learned from this particular book, then you might create cards representing various Teaching Formats, coffee breaks, etc., and ask attendees to combine the cards to create and evaluate a quick Skeleton in response to various constraints or goals. (If you'd like to use those cards, either personally or while teaching, we've made a free, downloadable set at: workshopsurvival.com/workshop-tools).

In terms of physically creating the cards, I usually start by just designing them in my slide software, and then printing them four-to-a-page on my printer and cutting them up. This takes forever and leads to cards which can't be easily shuffled, and which can only be used once before they're destroyed. But it's quick and easy to iterate, which is important for the first version of new teaching materials. After you've used them once or twice and are happy with how they work, you can invest the time in a polished design and send them off to a print shop to have them done on card stock (i.e. heavier weight paper). You can optionally spend a fortune on lamination and rounded corners and full-color double-sided cards, but it isn't really necessary. Unless I'm teaching a super-premium workshop, I typically just stick with single-sided, black and white, square corners, unlaminated. As long as it's on relatively rigid cardstock, it will still accomplish everything you need.

If you've trying to teach a list of things, consider delivering it as a deck of cards. Almost nobody uses cards in educational workshops, which is a real shame since they have so much potential. Cards are great!

Lessons learned:

- If you need to teach a "list of things", you can turn those things into a deck of cards for use in a number of fun exercises and games

Format: Lab time for working on their own projects

Lab Time is a large, unstructured block of time where attendees work at their own pace on their own projects, with you on hand to help if they get stuck. You can either provide them with a clear assignment or simply leave them to their own pursuits.

Lab Time is common in multi-day workshops where you've covered all the theory and need to start spending an increasing amount of time on actual practice. It's less common in shorter workshops (i.e. one day or less) where time is at a premium. If you ever took a university course in programming, architecture, design, art, fashion, ceramics, or any other hands-on discipline, you'll likely remember spending some portion of your class time in the lab, working on your own stuff.

The advantages are fairly obvious (folks enjoy working on their own projects and practice is helpful), so I'll focus on the limitations.

First, the energy level is difficult to control. It's a large, unstructured block of time. Attendees for whom the task is relevant will be fully engaged, whereas others will drift off and feel like it's a waste of an hour (or however much time). Second, students will progress at massively different paces. This is partly due to differences in understanding, and partly because some of their projects and ideas will be "easy" to move forwards, whereas others will be "difficult". This fragments the class and limits your ability to give class-wide instruction. Another issue is that lab time is highly help-dependent, and you'll only be able to handle a relatively small group by yourself before you need to start hiring additional teaching assistants. This makes lab time viable for high-priced premium courses but less so for low-priced and free ones.

There are a few ways to mitigate these problems. One is to force everyone to work on an example project instead of allowing them to work on their own. This means everyone will be able to make similar progress and makes it easier for you to help them (since they're all struggling with the same stuff). But it comes at a slight cost since people love the idea of moving forward with their own project during the workshop itself.

Another solution is to put a small piece of Lab Time immediately before a break. Folks who are engaged with the task will stay seated and happily working, whereas the less engaged can drift off and chat with each other over coffee, enjoying an extended break.

A related option is to finish the educational section of the workshop, wrap things up, and then continue with optional Lab Time for the participants who choose to continue working largely on their own, with a bit of help available if they need it. I sometimes use this structure in full-day workshops, where the hours up until lunch are tightly structured and educational, and the hours *after* lunch are an optional stretch of Lab Time.

(This structure needs to be communicated to attendees in advance, of course, so they can plan their day and bring their computers if necessary.) If you have the space and time, you can also schedule the Lab Time for a separate day and mention it as a "free bonus" when you announce your workshop.

One common trap with Lab Time is to depend too much on its output for the rest of the workshop. For example, when teaching web programming, you might first give them an hour to make the scaffolding for a simple portfolio website. And then you want them to spend the next hour doing design and layout. But because attendees diverge so much in their progress, many won't have finished the first step, which will then prevent them from beginning on the second. And others will have raced through both steps and then be twiddling their thumbs. The more of these steps you put in a row, the more fragmented and dissatisfied your audience will become. You can solve this by having loads of teaching assistants, or by providing a fresh start at each step for folks who got too far behind, or by treating Lab Time as a final, optional task instead of as a prerequisite for doing whatever's next.

Another trap, specifically for tasks which use a computer, is to expect folks to succeed in quickly downloading, installing, and getting comfortable with new software. People are somehow *terrible* at this, and the task will take at least an hour of your valuable time unless you're able to find a way to either massively simplify setup or to provide an already-equipped set of computers.

If you're teaching a lengthy course about hands-on skills, you can fill a surprising percentage of your schedule with relatively unstructured Lab Time. And your students will benefit from it, provided that you can work around the challenges listed above. After all, you can't learn pottery without getting your hands in the clay.

Lessons learned:

- Lab Time allows folks to apply what you've taught to their own projects, and is a great fit for long-form, skills-heavy topics
- If lab time is a core part of your event, you may need to bring extra facilitators to properly help everyone through their individual problems
- If the lab time is less crucial, consider making it optional by attaching it to an extended break, or by running it as a separate opt-in event

Appendix: An example of inventing, testing, and perfecting a new exercise

In this section, we'll walk through an example of designing an exercise which doesn't fit any of the "standard" Formats. As this sort of invention is a bit more open-ended than the rest of the book, I won't be able to tell you exactly what to do. But I *can* help you peek behind the curtain and see the choices I made along the way, and perhaps that's helpful too.

More than anything, I want you to remember that **going backwards is part of the process**. Although it would be great to be able to invent a perfect exercise on your first attempt, you typically won't even discover all the problems until after you've run it with a live audience. That's not failure; that's progress. Once you know about the problems, you go back and fix them for the next time. Design is iterative, and good design requires testing and refinement in front of real people.

If the workshop is high-stakes, and you need it to be perfect, then you can arrange some "practice sessions" with safe test audiences before the main event. Use your friends, your colleagues, a local meetup group, or whoever else you can get hold of. They don't need to sit through the whole workshop, but only the new exercises you're still trying to debug.

In this particular example, I wanted to run folks through a process for generating small, reliable business ideas. Instead of starting by picking an idea out of thin air, this process begins by first coming up with lists of "resources" that you already have access to, which can include things like:

- Your skills (e.g. design, programming, sales, cooking, recruitment, or whatever else)
- Potential partners (both individuals and businesses) who might help you out, plus whatever skills or other benefits they could offer
- The types of customers and industries which you understand and can find some way to get in touch with

Attendees then mix-and-match resources from these lists to get a whole assortment of little business ideas. Most of them are terrible, but some can be interesting, and it's a different way of thinking about business opportunities. Plus, I suspected that it would end up being a fun exercise and a nice energy boost.

So, the basic exercise structure is:

1. Generate lists of resources
2. Combine resources into ideas

Sounds simple enough. But there are still plenty of open questions:

- **Group size:** Should attendees brainstorm their resources individually or in groups? What about when they're combining ideas? Individually, in pairs, or in groups?
- **Where to write it down:** On worksheets, scrap paper, or sticky notes? Will folks want to save their ideas, or are the ideas just throwaways for the sake of the exercise?
- **Facilitation basics:** How should the groups be formed and how should the exercise be broken up and explained? How many intermediary steps are required to avoid any students getting lost or confused?
- **Variation:** How often (if at all) should groups be rearranged, and the rules be changed, to reduce Format Fatigue?
- **Timing and pacing:** Should this exercise feel "fast and frantic" or "slow and thoughtful"? How long do attendees spend brainstorming resources vs. combining them into possible business ideas? How much lecture do they need beforehand to understand the point of the exercise? How much time do we spend at the end to review what they've learned?
- **Repetition:** Do we repeat the exercise several times? If so, how many? What do we change (if anything) each time it repeats? Is the timing rigid, or can later repetitions be cut to use it as a Schedule Spring?

I got started by making a fairly arbitrary set of initial guesses. Here's what I came up with as my first attempt:

1. Individually, spend five minutes writing down all the resources you can think of from these three categories, on sticky notes.
2. Get into pairs.
3. From your combined lists: pick a customer, a skill, and a business partner. Write down a possible business idea which uses those ingredients, and then repeat. See how many ideas you can get in 2 minutes.
4. As a pair, mark your favorite ideas, and then "stand and share" about why you liked it.
5. Repeat the idea generation two more times, switching to a new partner each time (but keeping your list of resources the same).

Can you spot some of the problems? I didn't, so I ran it for the first time as written above. It wasn't a *total* failure, but it did have low energy, and lots of people got lost and confused. Here's are the problems I noticed after that first attempt:

1. **Drawing the owl:** In the very first step of list-writing, I had given them a long block of time to generate three different lists of resources. This was super confusing, since it combined three different tasks into a single exercise.
2. **Long, boring list-writing:** To make matters worse, the long stretch of individual work was a big drag on energy, which caused some folks to get off-track, stop working, and look at their phones.
3. **Repetitive idea generation:** Although switching partners was helpful for exposing everyone to fresh ideas and resources, the exact repetition three times in a row felt really bad.

4. **Physically moving the resource lists:** I had asked folks write their resources on sticky notes. But I was also asking folks to move around to find new partners, and it's not easy to physically transport a bunch of stickies.

Okay, so those are some big problems. (Incidentally, this is the sort of analysis you should do after every workshop, about every exercise and every section which ended up feeling less than perfect. This is the sort of stuff a workshop post-mortem should dredge up.) But don't despair! Now that I was aware of what was wrong, I was able to iterate the exercise to fix it

The first problem (drawing the owl) was solved by simply separating the list-writing task into three separate steps, each with a tighter timer and prompt.

Problems 2 and 3 (boring and repetitive tasks) were addressed with the same sort of reordering and variation that you'd use to fix a workshop's overall energy levels. First, I also interleaved the resource writing (R) with the idea generation (I). So instead of doing R-R-R-I-I-I, the new order became R-R-I-R-I-I. Beyond the obvious variation between R and I, this also made the first idea generation feel different from subsequent two repetitions, since the latter attempts had access to an extra list of resources. I also changed the facilitation of the third idea generation, asking folks to work in triplets instead of pairs and giving them five minutes instead of three, allowing them to go deeper now that they were more experienced with the task.

To solve the sticky note problem, I simply asked them to write their lists on a piece of paper divided into four columns (three for their resources, one for the resulting ideas). This also had the bonus of creating a high-value artefact that they could take home with them.

There were a few other minor points of friction with room setup and group formation which I eventually ironed out. By the third iteration, the exercise worked brilliantly: zero confusion, tight timings, and top-tier energy. (As pleasant surprise, the ideas weren't as silly as I had expected, and some of the attendees actually ended up forming businesses to pursue them.) Now that everybody could get through the exercise without getting confused, distracted, or lost, I no longer needed to spend my time running around doing 1-on-1 clarifications and interventions. And *that*, in turn, meant that the exercise could scale to support an arbitrarily large audience. Neat.

Exercise design is easier if you're willing to embarrass yourself a little bit. Sometimes the first crack at a bold new exercise is such a debacle that all you can do is to laugh it off and throw the whole thing in the bin. No biggie, it happens. And if that sort of result isn't an option, remember that you can eliminate the risk by either starting with a safe test audience, or by simply sticking to the tried and true Teaching Formats.

The biggest improvements in the example above came from simple stuff that we've already talked discussed: splitting a big prompt into pieces; interleaving different Formats to boost variation; varying and simplifying group formation. There's no mystical secret here... Just testing, observation, and iteration. The standard Teaching Formats are pretty much "off the shelf". But if you want to create brand new exercises and Formats, then you're going to have to put on your inventor hat and keep testing and iterating until it's brilliant.

Lessons learned:

- To invent an exercise from scratch, take a best guess at the facilitation details and then try it with a safe audience
- Identify spots with high facilitation friction, where folks get confused, or where the energy dips, and find a way to resolve them (e.g. with clearer prompts, alternating formats, or subdividing a large exercise into pieces)
- The next time you run it, look for problem areas yet again, and try more improvements
- Good job :)

Made in the USA
Middletown, DE
28 February 2024